THE
CHINESE
WAY IN
BUSINESS

"Do not be in too much of a hurry to get things done. Do not see only petty gains. If a man hurries too much, things will not be done well or thoroughly. If he sees only minor advantages nothing great is accomplished."

– Confucius

THE
CHINESE
WAY IN
BUSINESS

THE SECRETS OF SUCCESSFUL
BUSINESS DEALINGS IN CHINA

BOYÉ LAFAYETTE DE MENTE

TUTTLE Publishing

Tokyo | Rutland, Vermont | Singapore

Published by Tuttle Publishing, an imprint of Periplus Editions (HK) Ltd.

www.tuttlepublishing.com

Library of Congress Cataloging-in-Publication Data in process

ISBN 978-0-8048-4350-8

Distributed by

North America, Latin America & Europe
Tuttle Publishing
364 Innovation Drive
North Clarendon, VT 05759-9436 U.S.A.
Tel: 1 (802) 773-8930
Fax: 1 (802) 773-6993
info@tuttlepublishing.com
www.tuttlepublishing.com

Asia Pacific
Berkeley Books Pte. Ltd.
61 Tai Seng Avenue #02-12
Singapore 534167
Tel: (65) 6280-1330
Fax: (65) 6280-6290
inquiries@periplus.com.sg
www.periplus.com

Japan
Tuttle Publishing
Yaekari Building, 3rd Floor
5-4-12 Osaki, Shinagawa-ku
Tokyo 141 0032
Tel: (81) 3 5437-0171
Fax: (81) 3 5437-0755
sales@tuttle.co.jp
www.tuttle.co.jp

Indonesia
PT Java Books Indonesia
Kawasan Industri Pulogadung
Jl. Rawa Gelam IV No. 9
Jakarta 13930
Tel: (62) 21 4682-1088
Fax: (62) 21 461-0207
crm@periplus.co.id
www.periplus.com

First edition
17 16 15 14 13   10 9 8 7 6 5 4 3 2 1   1301RP

Printed in China

Contents

PART THREE

Doing Business in China

PART FOUR
Key Concepts in Chinese Business Practice

PART FIVE

Additional Business Vocabulary | 155

PART SIX

Glossary of Useful Terms | 165

PART SEVEN

Internet Gateways to China

PART EIGHT

Miscellaneous Information

PART NINE

Learning Some New Skills

The Land & the People

$\longrightarrow\!\!\!\diamond\!\!\!\longrightarrow$

One of the key aspects of doing business in China is the fact that business ethics and practices are strongly influenced by the cultures of the regional divisions—some of which are several times larger than individual American states and European countries.

Neither traditional nor modern China can be understood and dealt with effectively without taking into account its huge size and the ethnic, racial, religious, and cultural regions of the country.

REGIONS OF CHINA

In addition to the great north-south divisions of China, the country is further divided into seven regions—three in the south, three in the north, and one in the west.

In the south there is Southern China, Southeast China, and Southwest China. Southern China is made up of Hubei, Hunan, and parts of Zhejiang, Jiangxi, Shaanxi, and Anhui provinces. Shanghai, often listed as the most populous city in the world, is in this region. Southern China is also the most densely populated region in the country.

Southeast China, which is very hilly, includes the coastal provinces of Zhejian, Fujian, and Guangdong. The well-known city of Guangzhou (Canton) is the largest city in Guangdong province, of which the New Territories, Hong Kong, and Macao are a part. The two most widely spoken languages in this region are Cantonese and Amoy.

Southwest China consists of the provinces of Yunnan, Guizhou, Sichuan, and the autonomous region of Guangxi. Much of this huge area has very rugged terrain. Sichuan is especially noted for its scenic mountains, rivers, and beautiful valleys— plus its spicy food.

The Chinese consider Qinghai, the autonomous region that borders Sichuan on the northwest, as their wild west. It is remote, made up of mountains, desert, and grasslands, and is thinly populated. The capital, Chengdu at an altitude of 7,380 feet (2,250 meters), is filled with non-Chinese minorities— Mongols, Kazaks, Hui, and Tibetans that give it an exotic non-Chinese appearance.

Turpan, in central Xinjiang (which is even farther west and the largest autonomous region in China), still has its grape arbors and one occasionally sees donkeys in the streets, and has been described by Western visitors as like something out of ancient times. The city is both the hottest and lowest city in China—500 feet (150 meters) below sea level, with summertime temperatures that regularly go well above the 100°F (38° C) mark.

Northern China is bounded on the north by the Great Wall, on the east by the Huai River, on the south by the Tsinling Mountains, and on the west by Inner Mongolia. This region is frequently compared to North America's Great Plains insofar as terrain and climate are concerned.

The northwest region of China begins with the Taihung Mountains in Shanxi province and extends to the far west of Inner Mongolia. It is the homeland of many of the Aryan peoples of China, including the Kazakhs, Kirghiz, Hui, and Uyghurs.

The northeast region is the area that was formerly known as Manchuria; it borders North Korea and a great swatch of Russian Siberia. China's seventh region lumps Inner Mongolia and Tibet together.

THE HAN PEOPLE

The largest racial and ethnic group in China is generally referred to as the *Han* (Hahn) Chinese, Han being the name given to the indigenous group that made its home in the valley of the Yellow River and is credited with being the founders of Chinese civilization. In addition to this huge core group, China has 55 recognized minorities, mostly living in the outlying southern provinces and the western autonomous regions.

China's largest minority group is the Zhuang, some fourteen million, who are concentrated in the Guangxi Zhuang Autonomous Region on the southern border. The Zhuang look very much like the Han Chinese, but their native language is related to Thai.

The Uygurs, who number well over six million and are another of China's largest minorities, are more related to the Turks than to the Han Chinese. Their native language closely resembles Turkish, their written script is Arabic, and their religion is Islam. Primarily Caucasian in appearance, their ancestral homeland is the plateaus and mountains of Xinjiang in China's far west. The Hui people, numbering approximately two million, live in the Ningxia Hui Autonomous Region of Northwest China, making up about one-third of the population in this area. They are Muslims.

THE YUNNAN MENAGERIE

Not surprisingly, a significant percentage of China's minority peoples are found in the far southern mountainous province of Yunnan. A total of twenty-four ethnic groups live in this region, or almost half of all the ethnic minorities in the country. Thirteen of these groups are found in just the Xishuangbanna region of the province, which borders Laos, Vietnam, and Burma.

Xishuangbanna is a subtropical area made up of fertile plains, hills, and mountains that boasts one-fourth of all the wild animal life in the country and one-sixth of its plant species. Elephants, leopards, tigers, monkeys and an incredible array of birds inhabit the region along with its amazing variety of people.

The ethnic minorities of Xishuangbanna outnumber the Han Chinese in the region. The largest ethnic group is the Dai, an ancient race related to the Thai, who are devout Buddhists. Other groups include the Hani, Bulang, Lahu, Akha, and Jinuo. Each group has its own language, distinctive tribal customs, and elaborate native wear. And there are extraordinary physical differences in the people despite their proximity to each other.

Large numbers of China's minorities, situated on the outer edge of the country in generally remote areas, maintain their traditional lifestyles of farming and herding, following customs that are thousands of years old.

CHINA'S PROVINCES

Anhui: 55,000 square miles (140,000 sq.km); population 50 million; capital: Hefei.

Fujian: 47,000 square miles (121,700 sq.km); population 26 million; capital: Fuzhou.

Gansu: 174,000 square miles (450,000 sq.km); population 20 million; capital: Lanzhou.

Guangdon: 82,000 square miles (212,000 sq.km); population 61 million; capital: Guangzhou.

Guizhou: 67,000 square miles (174,000 sq.km); population 28 million; capital: Guiyang.

Hainan: 13,000 square miles (34,000 sq.km); population 6 million; capital: Haikou.

Heibei: 72,000 square miles (187,700 sq.km); population 54 million; capital: Shijiazhuang.

Heilungjiang: 181,000 square miles (469,000 sq.km); population 33.1 million; capital: Harbin.

Henan: 65,000 square miles (169,000 sq.km); population 75 million; capital: Zhenzhou.

Hubei: 72,000 square miles (187,000 sq.km); population 48 million; capital: Wuhan.

Hunan: 81,000 square miles (210,000 sq.km); population 55.1 million; capital: Changsha.

Jiangsu: 39,000 square miles (102,600 sq.km); population 60.2 million; capital: Nanjing.

Jiangxi: 64,000 square miles (166,600 sq.km); population 32 million; capital: Nanchang.

Jilin: 69,000 square miles (180,000 sq.km); population 23 million; capital: Changchun.

Liaoning: 56,000 square miles (145,740 sq.km); population 36.3 million: capital: Shenyang.

Quinghai: 278,000 square miles (720,000 sq.km); population 4 million; capital: Xining.

Shaanxi: 76,000 square miles (195,800 sq.km); population 29.1 million; capital: Xi'an.

Shandong: 59,000 square miles (153,300 sq.km); population 74 million; capital: Jinan.

Shanxi: 60,000 square miles (156,000 sq.km); population 25.5 million; capital: Taiyuan.

Sichuan: 220,000 square miles (570,000 sq.km); population 100 million; capital: Chengdu.

Zhejiang: 39,000 square miles (101,800 sq.km); population 38.9 million; capital: Hangzhou.

CITIES WITH PROVINCIAL STATUS

Beijing: 6,500 square miles (16,800 sq.km) in area; estimated population 10 million.

Shanghai: 2,400 square miles (6,186 sq.km) in area; estimated population 12.7 million.

Tianjian: 4,000 square miles (11,000 sq.km) in area; estimated population 7.5 million.

AUTONOMOUS REGIONS

Guangxi Zhuang: 88,800 square miles (230,000 sq.km) in area; estimated population 41 million; capital: Nanning.

Inner Mongolia: 425,000 square miles (1,100,000 sq.km) in area; estimated population 21 million; capital: Hohhot.

Ningxia Hui: 255,000 square miles (660,000 sq.km) in area; estimated population 4.5 million; capital: Yinchuan.

Tibet: 464,000 square miles (1,200,000 sq.km) in area; estimated population 0.2 million; capital: Lhasa.

Xinjiang Uygur: 618,000 square miles (1,600,000 sq.km) in area; estimated population 14 million; capital: Turpan.

THE LANGUAGES OF CHINA

Chinese is a family of languages like the Romance languages of Europe. China's famous "dialects" (Cantonese, Shanghaiese, Fukienese, etc.) are not mutually understandable and are therefore just as much "real" languages as Spanish and Italian.

Altogether there are ten major languages in China, including Mandarin, Cantonese, Shanghaiese, Fukienese, Hokkien, Hakka, and Chin Chow, plus several dozen minority languages, including a number in the far west that are related to Turkish.

Historically, the vitally important difference between the main family of Chinese languages and the Roman family was that there is just one writing system for all of the major Chinese languages. Despite the fact that the languages have many different words with different pronunciations, they all used the same ideographic writing system in which all of the individual ideograms making up the writing system have the same meaning. They are just pronounced differently in the different languages. *This means the Chinese could read the different languages without being able to speak them.*

It is this remarkable factor that held the core group of Chinese people together over the millennia, despite long periods of political separation and physical isolation from each other. This writing system was standardized in the 3rd Century B.C. and with the exception of simplification in the number of strokes in commonly used ideograms it has remained virtually the same ever since. Today's less-stroke version is officially referred to as Simplified Chinese.

At the fall of the Qing Dynasty in 1911 China did not have a national language or an education system that could teach the proper sounds of any of the languages. In 1913 the new government decided a national language should be established. A group of scholars chosen by government officials made the decision that Mandarin, the language of the north, would be the national language.

A set of phonetic symbols were created and a dictionary was published. However, this dictionary did not resemble Mandarin as it was spoken because it retained the pronunciations of the southern languages. Only one person could speak the language set down in the dictionary—the native Wu speaker who created it. It was not until 1932 that a dictionary based on the pronunciation and speech of Mandarin, the language of the Beijing area, came about.

The originally projection was that Mandarin would become the national standard within 100 years, and that by 2030 the whole nation would be unified linguistically. When Mao took over China in 1949 one of the things he did was to mandate that Mandarin would be taught in all schools as the primary language—something that had not been done.

However, because of the sheer size of China and the number of various languages spoken, teaching everyone Mandarin and making it the national standard has been a long journey, and even now most of the native languages and dialects are thriving. In many schools, classes are given in the local language and Mandarin is studied as a separate language (much like a foreign language class) for use when speaking to non-locals.

Grammatically, Chinese resembles English—subject, verb, object—but there are no other similarities. Chinese words are made up of one, two, three, or more "syllables," each of which requires an ideogram or character to write. The majority of modern Chinese words have two syllables and require two characters to write.

All languages are continuously changing, but since 1976 Mandarin Chinese has changed more than most because of the rapid influx of new products and new ideas for which there were no traditional terms. These changes are so rapid and in so many areas that even the most accomplished translators and interpreters are unable to keep current on everything.

There are also significant differences between spoken and written Chinese and between informal and "official" Chinese. Informal spoken Chinese is very loose and casual. In formal or "official" situations, spoken Chinese becomes very stylized, very refined, and requires great skill and experience to use properly. Written Chinese has even more levels of use and, in the case of government propaganda or official communications, is charged with special meanings and nuances that are difficult or impossible for non-Chinese to fully grasp.

It is also common for the Chinese to speak in flowery, exaggerated terms that can be misleading to someone not familiar with this form of cultural expression. Further, it is also a deeply ingrained Chinese characteristic to speak in vague, often ambiguous terms as part of the process of not directly committing themselves to anything, while also protecting both their "face" and the "face" of others.

Irene Park, an American cross-cultural communications expert with years of experience in China, once said: "Chinese is not designed to clearly, concisely communicate information. It is a means of expressing feelings, emotions, and 'polite escapes.'"

Park explained that "polite escapes," which she said make up approximately eighty percent of Chinese language usage, were ploys to avoid accepting responsibility or making commitments. "If you ask someone, 'Is this white or black?' a typical response is, 'Well, it isn't very gray.' If you extend this kind of reaction to virtually all other areas of business, you have a pretty good idea of the problems involved in communicating with Chinese."

While this way of using Chinese has diminished, particularly in the business community, there are still significant differences in the way language is used. It is important for the foreign business person in China to be wary of engaging in a lot of loose chatter and, particularly during business discussions, to use simple, straightforward terms that lend themselves to direct translation and reduce the possibility of misunderstandings. The habit of incorporating jokes and vague references during speeches and presentations should especially be avoided during the early stages of any relationship.

Only extended exposure to the Chinese way of using language allows one to understand what is really being said. For example, when someone says that something is "inconvenient," the true meaning is most likely that nothing is going to happen or that it is impossible so you may as well forget it. The Chinese habitually use "maybe" and "perhaps" to preface statements that they mean categorically. At the same time, during negotiations there are occasions when these conditional terms are used in their "proper" sense, leaving room for further discussions.

It is also important to keep in mind that while Mandarin—*Putunghua* (Poo-toong-hwah) or "Common Language"—is the official language of China and is the official language of education in the country's twenty-one provinces and five autonomous regions, Cantonese, Hakka, and several other Chinese languages are still widely spoken.

Mandarin Chinese is "straightforward" and less complex than many other languages. Some consider it easier to learn than many languages because it does not have verb tenses, conjugations, declensions, inflections, genders, or moods. Most of the rules of Chinese grammar have to do with word order rather than word changes. However, expatriate businesspeople who have gained considerable fluency in the language say it is far from easy to master.

The biggest problem for most people who undertake the study of Mandarin is the existence of tones that change the meanings of words. Mandarin, having only four tones (Cantonese has nine), is easier than the other related languages which have more tones. The four tones of Mandarin are high level, rising, falling-then-rising, and falling.

Another problem faced by foreigners studying Mandarin results from the fact that it apparently has more words that sound exactly alike than any other language. An attempt to remedy this situation was made around A.D. 500 when a tonal system was adopted, but the problem remains. There are hundreds of words that have dozens of meanings. One of the most often quoted examples is the word "*I*" [ee], which has sixty-nine meanings, some of which are *city, ant, soap*, and *barbarian*.

This situation has contributed to a national habit of punning. Many Chinese constantly spice their conversation with esoteric puns that make the language especially difficult for foreign students to understand—but are an extraordinary vehicle for humor when one knows it well.

Early Western missionaries in China devised a number of systems for writing Chinese phonetically in Roman letters. None of these systems was a true representation of the correct pronunciation of the languages involved, which caused a great deal of confusion.

In 1951 the government of the People's Republic of China began working on a new phonetic alphabet for Mandarin, which had been designated as the official language of the country. This new system, called *pinyin (peen-een)*, or "phonetic transcription," was introduced in 1979. In this system all vowels are pronounced as they are in Latin, but there are several consonants that have totally unrelated pronunciations and, phonetically speaking, make no sense at all as far as English is concerned. See the pronunciation guide below.

PRONUNCIATION GUIDE

(The official phonetic alphabet for Mandarin)

Pinyin	As in:	Pinyin	As in:
a	far	p	par
b	be	q	cheek
c	similar to ts in its	r	rzh
ch	church	s	so
d	do	sh	shore
e	her	t	top
ei	way	u	too

Pinyin	As in:	Pinyin	As in:
f	foot	v	used only in foreign words and some dialects
g	go		
h	her		
i	eat	w	want
j	jeep	x	she
k	kind	y	yet
l	land	z	zoo (zu) sound
m	me	zh	pronounced j (jump)
n	no		
o	law		

Learning how to say a dozen or so things in Mandarin can go a long way in China. *Ni hao* (nee how), for example, has several meanings: "Hello," "Good morning," "Good afternoon," "Good evening," "How are you?"

USEFUL EXPRESSIONS

Thank you	Xie Xie *(shay shay)*
Very good	Hen hao *(hern how)*
Tasty	Hen hao chi *(hern how chee)*
Cheers (toast)	Ganbei *(ghan-bay)*
Friendship	Youyi *(yoe-eee)*
How are you?	Ni hao ma? *(nee how mah?)*

Numbers are vital in basic communication, and fortunately the Chinese counting system is simple and similar to the Roman system. It is made up of combinations of elements beginning with zero, plus an additional key word for one hundred, one thousand, ten thousand, and so on. Eleven, for example, is ten plus one; twenty is two tens; fifty is five tens.

0 ling *(leng)*

1 yi *(eee)*

2 er *(rr)*

3 san *(sahn)*

4 si *(suh)*

5 wu *(woo)*

6 liu *(lee-yu)*

7 qi *(chee)*

8 ba *(ba)*

9 jiu *(jee-yu)*

10 shi *(shur)*

11 shi-yi *(shur-eee)*

12 shi-er *(shur-rr)*

13 shi-san *(shur-sahn)*

14 shi-si *(shur-suh)*

15 shi-wu *(shur-woo)*

16 shi-liu *(shur-lee-yu)*

17 shi-qi *(shur-chee)*

18 shi-ba *(shur-bah)*

19 shi-jiu *(shur-jee-yu)*

20 er-shi *(rr-shur)*

21 er-shi-yi *(rr-shur-yee)*

25 er-shi-wu *(rr-shur-woo)*

30 san-shi *(sahn-shur)*

31 san-shi-yi *(san-shur-eee)*

38 san-shi-ba *(sahn-shur-bah)*

40 si-shi *(suh-shur)*

50 wu-shi *(woo-shur)*

100 yi-bai *(eee-buy)*

200 er-bai *(rr-buy)*

500 wu-bai *(woo-buy)*

1,000 yi-qian *(eee-chee-inn)*

10,000 wan *(wahn)*

A LITTLE LESSON IN CANTONESE

Cantonese is the principal Chinese language of Hong Kong, Macao, and the surrounding region. It has nine tones, five more tones than Mandarin, and is therefore more difficult to learn. It is certainly a noisier language.

Foreigners first exposed to Cantonese often believe the speakers are engaged in a serious shouting match. Having to clearly enunciate the different tones makes it necessary to emphasize them loudly. Here are a few useful words and numbers (which you do not have to shout out to be understood!).

Good morning / Jo san (*Joe sahn*)
Good night / Jo tau (*Joe tah-uu*)
Goodbye / Joy geen (*Joy gheen*)
Thank you (for service) / M'goy (*Mm-goy*)
Thank you (for gift) / Doh jay (*dor chay*)
Yes / Hai *(Hie)*
No / M'hai *(Mm-hie)*

1 yaht	18 sahp baht
2 yee	19 sahp gau (*sahp gow*)
3 sahm	20 yee sahp
4 say	21 yee sahp yaht
5 ng *(nng)*	22 yee sahp yee
6 luk	23 yee sahp sahm
7 chat	24 yee sahp say
8 baht	25 yee sahp ng
9 gau *(gow)*	30 sahm sahp
10 sahp	40 say sahp
11 sahp yaht	50 ng sahp *(nng sahp)*
12 sahp yee	100 yaht bahk
13 sahp sahm	200 yee bahk
14 sahp say	300 sahm bahk
15 sahp ng *(sahp nng)*	400 say bahk
16 sahp luk	500 ng bahk *(nng bahk)*
17 sahp chat	

CHINA'S SECRET CODE

Referring to *Hanyu* (Hahn-yuu), the languages of China, as China's secret code is a bit of stretch but is intended to emphasize a key factor in China's historical and present-day relations with other people.

The point is that the existence of ten major Chinese languages (and dozens of minority languages and regional dialects) along with one of the most complex of all writing systems has traditionally served as the "Great Wall" of China—a wall that has helped keep the country isolated, insulated, and exclusive until modern times.

In the past so few Westerners learned Chinese (except for dedicated missionaries) that there was very little communication between ordinary Chinese and Westerners—and the bulk of that was with Chinese who had learned English or some other foreign language. As a result very few Westerners were ever able to fully understanding Chinese culture.

This failing is gradually being remedied, as more and more non-Chinese are learning Mandarin—and this includes Americans, who traditionally ignored language learning as an important skill.

But the "language wall" that has obscured China for so many millennia is far from being breached, and continues to present a challenge to the rest of the world.

Sociologists call Mandarin Chinese a "high context" language to indicate that there is more to the message than just the words being spoken or written. You have to pay attention to the situation, environmental factors, and history to understand the real meaning. Sometimes it is more important to listen to what they are not saying.

CHINESE NAMES

Chinese family and given names are often confusing to the foreign visitor. Altogether there are some 438 Chinese surnames, with 30 of these being double, clan names. The three most common family names are Wang (wahng), Zhang (Jahng), and Li (Lee). Some 10 percent of the total population is named Zhang, or well over one hundred million, which gives a very good indication of the problems of keeping people and their names straight. Sixty percent of all Chinese have only nineteen surnames; 90 percent have only one hundred surnames—all of which are remnants of ancient clan names.

To help diminish both the appearance and reality of this problem, I have chosen in this book to follow the Western practice of placing the first or given name first, which may seem rather odd where well-known names like Zedong Mao or Kai-shek Chiang are concerned, but it soon "makes sense" and feels natural.

When Chinese names are written in Roman letters in Hong Kong and Taiwan, a hyphen generally separates the first name and the "middle" name (Zi-yang). On mainland China, the custom is to run the two names together as if they were one (Ziyang). The explanation is that this is done to prevent foreigners from thinking that the second middle name is the last name.

Traditionally all Chinese received a "milk name" at birth, a "book name" upon entering school, and a "style" or "great name" upon marriage. The "milk name" was normally used by members of the family and very close friends. The "book name" was used by teachers and school friends. Both parents and relatives would also use the individual's new "style" name after marriage.

In feudal days, scholars also commonly assumed a "studio name," which they used in signing their works.

No doubt because of the profusion of identical names, many Chinese ended up with nicknames often associated with their physical appearance or characteristics. When the exodus from China began in the 1800s, Chinese who lived overseas generally adopted Western first names in addition to their Chinese given names.

It is customary to address Chinese by their last name, using the title Miss, Mrs., or Mr. until you become good friends or they let you know the nickname or Western name they prefer to be called. In rank-and-status conscious China, job and profession-related titles are especially important as badges of respect and recognition. People liked to be called by their titles. One reason for this might be the fact that so many people have the same family names. When there are 100 million Zhangs, who could get excited over being called Mr. or Mrs. Zhang?

It is common, for example, to call any tradesperson or skilled person Shi Fu *(Shur Fuu)* or "master craftsperson," whether the individual is a carpenter, electrician, plumber, chauffeur, or cook. Traditionally, old people who have no work-related title were commonly called Lao *(Lough)*, which is more or less the equivalent of "Honorable Old One." Younger people with no identifiable name or job title were addressed as Xiao *(She-ow)*, or "Honorable Young One." Lao and Xiao could also be used as Mr. or Miss in front of family names.

The Chinese themselves generally address each other by the family name and an appropriate title, or by both the family name and full given name together, with the family name first—e.g., Lijiqi *(Lee-jee-chee)*. The obvious reason for this custom is that it helps distinguish all the Zhangs, Lees, and Zhous from each other.

Some additional common surnames are Cai, Cheng, Deng, Ding, Du, Feng, Gao, Gong, Gou, Han, He, Hu, Jiang, Lei, Liang, Li, Liu, Ma, Mah, Mao, Peng, Qian, Sun, Tang, Wang, Wei, Wen, Wu, Xu, Yao, Ye, Zhan, Zhou, Zhu.

The Chinese for family name is jiazu xìngshì (*jah-zuu sheeng-shur*). First name is míngzì (*meeng-zee*).

Return of the "Central Kingdom"

Chinese influence is being felt around the world in virtually every country on a scale that makes the post-World War II emergence of Japan as an economic superpower seem piddling by comparison.

There are demographic, economic, and cultural reasons why the Chinese are playing an increasingly significant role in the affairs of the world and will play an even more fundamental role in the future—reasons that no other country can match, and this makes the story of the return of the "Central Kingdom" of special interest and importance.

From the beginning of China's history as a nation-state until 1976 when Zedong Mao, founder of the People's Republic of China, died both the thinking and behavior of ordinary people were controlled by dictatorial government edicts and deeply embedded cultural beliefs that prevented them from thinking and behaving as individuals.

Ages ago members of China's ruling class created extraordinary inventions (the compass, gunpowder, paper, printing) along with technological innovations in architecture, engineering, arts, and crafts, but these amazing and far-reaching accomplishments did not result in emotional, intellectual, or spiritual freedom for the bulk of the population.

Over the millennia there were also incursions into China's heartland by outsiders but all were eventually absorbed into the mainstream of Chinese life and transformed by the power of the traditional culture.

Traditional China, with all of its hidebound bureaucracy and limitations on the thinking and behavior of the people, survived until the beginning of the 20th century.

STUDENT UPRISINGS

It was not until the coming of Westerners who had gone through the Industrial Revolution that the traditional culture of China came under serious attack. This encounter with the West led to a series of student uprisings, civil rebellions, and finally a revolution that ended the reign of the Imperial Court in 1911.

After the downfall of the Imperial Court sporadic fighting between Imperialists and Nationalists continued until 1927 when Zedong Mao launched his Communist revolution against both the Nationalist and Imperialist forces. This struggle was still going on in 1937 when Japan invaded China, resulting in the Nationalists and the Communists joining forces to fight the Japanese.

When Japan was defeated by the Allies and withdrew its forces from China the Communists and Nationalists renewed their civil war. In 1948, with massive support from the Soviet Union, Mao's Communist forces began a major campaign to totally destroy the Nationalist army, led by Gen. Kai-shek Chiang who was supported by the United States.

Despite aid from the U.S., Chiang and his followers were no match for the Communists, and to avoid complete destruction of his forces Chiang and the remnants of his army, with many of their families in tow, fled to Taiwan in 1949, leaving Mao master of the mainland.

MAO AS THE NEW EMPEROR

Zedong Mao was a brilliant strategist as well as a powerful writer and poet who resembled the warlords of an earlier time, but his vision for a new China knew no bounds. He began a crash program to destroy the ancient culture that had ruled the country for more than four thousand years, and rebuild a new society based on Communist ideology.

Some of the reforms instituted by Mao were admirable and positive. He made women equal with men under the law; launched land reforms that made many farmers owners of their own tiny fields; made it mandatory that Mandarin (the language of Beijing and the northern area of China) be taught in all schools as the national language, and more.

But his efforts from 1958 to 1962 to modernize the economy and turn China into a world-class industrial and nuclear power virtually overnight—epitomized by what he called the "Great Leap Forward"—was an abject failure resulting in a famine that caused the death of over 20 million people, unimaginable suffering for more millions, and a virtually complete breakdown in the economy. Commenting on this staggering number of deaths Mao later said: "The peasants are like grass. Mow them down and they spring up again!"

THE CULTURAL REVOLUTION

In 1966, in a last-ditch effort to stave off complete failure of his "Great Leap Forward," Mao initiated what he called "The Great Proletarian Cultural Revolution"—a campaign to literally eradicate all vestiges of the traditional culture and society and rebuild the country as a Marxist-Leninist paradise. To help promote this revolution, his Communist cohorts, led by Piao Lin, published a small book made up of quotations from his many speeches and writings on his philosophy and plans for remaking China.

Entitled *Quotations from Chairman Mao Zedong*, this little red leather-covered book quickly became the "cult bible" of the Communist movement, selling 700 million copies and turning Mao into a kind of god-figure.

Mao turned the vanguard of his cultural revolution over to the students of the country, directing them to form a huge number of "Red Guard" groups to carry out his goals.

The students—by this time angry and disillusioned by the chaos around them—began a 10-year long campaign that became an orgy of humiliation, torture, death, imprisonment, and slave labor for members of the educated class. Children were induced to become spies, turning their parents in for such things as owning books and having eye glasses. Libraries, museums, schools, and religious artifacts were burned. Extraordinary efforts were made to eliminate all references to the teachings of Confucius.

Millions of city dwellers were sent to the countryside without advance preparation to work as peasants, with millions of families separated from each other. Married couples were sent to different parts of the country and were allowed to see each only 12 days each year. Huge numbers of three-generation families were required to live in single rooms.

No one was immune to the rampages of the Red Guards and their backers in the Communist government. Even Xiaoping Deng who had been a lifelong ally of Mao and a ranking member of the Communist Party was purged from his high position and exiled to the countryside. His son was thrown from an upper storey window by Red Guards and crippled for life.

The so-called Cultural Revolution did not end until Mao died in 1976, by which time his reputation as an infallible god had become irreparably tainted. Shocked into some semblance of rationality, the ruling members of the Communist Party recalled Xiaoping Deng from his exile and made him the paramount leader of the country.

Far more open-minded and pragmatic than Mao (which was what got him exiled in the first place), Deng began promoting the reconstruction of China along capitalistic lines after viewing the amazing economic success of Shenzhen near Hong Kong. He picked up on the "to get rich is glorious" concept—apparently originated by a lower ranking Party member—making it the new national slogan…and the rest, as the saying goes, is history.

But the memories of the tragedy inflicted on China by Mao and the Red Guards was to forever change the mindset of most Chinese. From 1976 on the stories told by survivors of the labor camps and prisons were beyond the imagination of most people. Many of the Red Guards, by then in their 20s and early 30s, had become disillusioned with the revolution and regretted their actions.

One of the unintended consequences of this incredible period in China's history was that it turned most people against the Communist ideology, and from then on most of the urban population who were members of the Party remained members because that was often the only way they could get and keep jobs.

THE REMAKING OF CHINA

The new China that was to arise from the death and destruction inflicted upon the country by Mao was unlike anything ever seen before. For the first time in the history of the Chinese people they had the freedom to help themselves as individuals. Millions of them set out to do just that despite the extraordinary restrictions and handicaps placed on them by the ruling Communist Party.

In an incredible demonstration of the power of even limited personal freedom, the Chinese, their pent-up energy released for the first time in the history of the country, began an all-out effort to build new lives for themselves without thinking about political labels.

This amazing march to affluence by some 300 million urban Chinese along the eastern coast was aided by thousands of rich Chinese who had taken up residence in the United States, Hong Kong, Indonesia, Macau, Malaysia, the Philippines, Singapore, Taiwan, and Thailand, had used their unique culture and talents to prosper, and chose to invest heavily in their homeland.

THE EDUCATION BLITZKRIEG

The Chinese were among the first people on the planet to institutionalize and ritualize education for a significant proportion of the population, creating a class that ruled the country for more than three thousand years. This instilled in all Chinese the knowledge that the only road to wealth and power was through education.

In the early 1980s China's new leaders established a policy designed to transform the country's education system into one that emphasized science, math, the English language, and foreign cultures. Since that time large numbers of Chinese students have been educated to compete with the outside world on Western terms—and to win.

This policy included building new colleges and universities, dramatically increasing the number of graduates in math and science—and building an infrastructure that included state-of-the-art airports, highways, and a high-speed train network—all key parts of modernizing and internationalizing China's economy.

The education network the Chinese created in less than a decade made it the largest in the world—an expansion Yale University President Richard Levin described as without precedent in any country.

In addition to the millions of younger Chinese who have since been educated in China to compete with the outside world, hundreds of thousands have also studied abroad where they honed their cross-cultural and language skills and earned degrees in business administration and business-oriented subjects.

While traditional Chinese etiquette and ethics is basically incompatible with the Western style business environment that has emerged in China, it has not disappeared and continues to influence virtually all areas of business. It is therefore important and often vital that foreign businesspeople interacting with their Chinese counterparts and government officials be aware of the elements of traditional Chinese culture that continue to influence their thinking and behavior in day-to-day management and particularly in such matters as long-term planning and investment and in the overall contribution of a particular product or technology to China's national interests.

One thing that is especially important for Western businesspeople to keep in mind is that the underlying philosophy of government agencies in China is to approve of projects whose benefits to the Chinese side are significant if not primary. This nationalistic goal has a direct impact on the origin and nature of the ethics Chinese bureaucrats use in making decisions.

A NEW BREED OF PEOPLE

Urban Chinese born from 1980 on grew up in a new world— a world so different from the past that they became a new breed of people, in many ways identical to freewheeling Americans in their lifestyles and appearance.

By 1986, just 10 years after Mao's death and the end of the Cultural Revolution, there were millions of entrepreneurs in China, thousands of whom had become millionaires, and the number of wealthy people was growing exponentially.

By 2000 Chinese cities in the eastern portion of the country had modern and futuristic buildings and high-end shops and stores that were astounding to even the most sophisticated visitors. For those who had not seen China since the 1976-1986 decade the changes were mind-boggling.

Dr. Wendy Liu, an author, translator, and consultant on the Chinese economy who was born in China and raised during the infamous Cultural Revolution [1966-1976], has presented a powerful portrait of fundamental changes that took place in China between 1979 and 2009.

She noted that in 1979 the private sector was virtually non-existent. Seventy percent of the workforce was in agriculture, working under the commune system. Most urban Chinese worked for the state or state-owned enterprises, with only 0.2 percent of them employed in private enterprise. At that time few urban Chinese owned their homes.

By 2009 homeownership among urban Chinese had soared past 80 percent. That was higher than American homeownership, which was at 67 percent, according to the U.S. Census Bureau.

By the end of 2009 China was primarily a private economy, with the private sector accounting for 70 percent of its GDP and employing over 75 percent of the urban workforce—not that different from the U.S. where over 10 percent of the population worked in the public sector.

As for China's agricultural employment, urbanization had reduced it to some 40 percent of the workforce, which was still shrinking. With the communes long gone, Chinese farmers worked for themselves but most of them still did not own the land they farmed, although a new government policy allowed them to lease their contracted farmland and transfer land-use rights.

In 2010 China's GNP passed that of Japan, making it the second largest economy on the planet. The 2010 *Hurun Rich List* (China's equivalent of the Forbes list) noted that 271 of China's 1,000 richest people were billionaires. The richest of the rich had a fortune of $11 billion. Thousands of Chinese were millionaires, and it was said that 10 percent of China's richest individuals owned 45 percent of the country's wealth—a percentage much higher than what existed in the U.S.

That same year China also bypassed Japan in the number of annual patent applications, with a total of 391,177—up from

50,000 applications in 2000—making it second only to the U.S. That was a portent of the innovative and inventive genius of the Chinese that was to mark the coming future of the country.

THE POWER OF TRADITION

The degree of the Westernization and modernization of Chinese management varies with the individuals, the companies, the government agencies, as well as the product and service categories concerned. In all matters of substance the power of China's traditional culture continues to influence what goes on in the country.

The traditional work-ethic and the Chinese respect for the power of education have been retained, and they continue to be influenced by age-old customs and traditional forms of behavior in their personal affairs—and as old China business hands repeatedly caution newcomers, the Chinese do not separate their business and personal life.

Another traditional trait that has survived into modern times is the extraordinary ability of the Chinese to entertain, please, and distract foreigners. This is a factor that Western businesspeople, diplomats, and politicians should keep in mind when they are dealing with their Chinese counterparts.

THOUGHT-CONTROL

There are some invidious leftovers from the past in the policies of China's reigning Communist Party. The government policy regarding information and free speech is designed to maintain what it refers to as "harmonious relations" throughout the economy and society.

What is vital to keep in mind is that a harmonious society in its official Chinese government context does not include freedom of speech or opposition to the ruling powers. The government goes to extreme lengths to prevent the dissemination of information that might contribute to weakening its control.

EXODUS OF THE RICH

By the end of the first decade of the 21st century ongoing government restrictions on the freedoms of the Chinese people had precipitated a remarkable phenomenon—the exodus of thousands of the country's well-to-do families to the United States and Canada, and the investment of billions of dollars abroad by wealthy individuals.

This phenomenon was the reverse of what happened in the 1800s when millions of Chinese fled from the country to escape extreme poverty and the total lack of opportunity to change their lives.

Among the reasons given by the wealthy who moved their families and their assets abroad: distrust of the Chinese government; to escape the law that Chinese couples can have only one child; to send their children to better schools; to escape such laws as the one that returns property you have bought and paid for to the state after 70 years, and the simple but powerful desire to have more freedom to do and say what they want.

The innate desire of the Chinese people to be free of onerous government regulations and the government policy of limiting these freedoms are obviously incompatible. What this means for China will help shape the future of the world.

One glaringly obvious result of the growing affluence of many Chinese is that the wealthier they become the less "Chinese" they become in their thinking and management practices.

CHINA'S NEW HYBRID ETHICS

Chinese ethics today consist of a hybrid of traditional values and behavior, which can be defined as primarily based on human feelings and human relations, and American or Western values and behavior, which are more or less based on facts, logical thinking, and making a profit.

Which set of values and which form of behavior is in play depends on the age of the individuals, their gender, their class, their educational background, their work experience, and the setting. Younger urban Chinese are typically far more Western than traditional Chinese in their values and behavior, especially when interacting with foreigners.

Virtually all "Westernized" Chinese are capable of switching back-and-forth between traditional Chinese ethics and Western ethics, depending on the circumstances. Some circumstances favor—or require—traditional Chinese values and behavior, while others are best served by a typical Western approach.

This dual set of values and behavior serves the Chinese especially well in their dealings with foreigners, while often putting foreigners at a disadvantage. The challenge facing foreigners in China is to be knowledgeable enough about the traditional mindset and behavior of the Chinese to know when that set of rules is in play and how to react in an effective and acceptable manner.

It is not easy—especially for "mainstream" Americans—to achieve this level of ability because we have had little or no experience in dealing with cultural differences and often disregard or ignore them as being irrational or unimportant. The traditional American attitude has been that all foreigners should do things the American way. In China that can have unintended and undesirable results.

It is important to keep in mind that Western style ethics often do not fit the expectations or requirements of the Chinese because in China family and group obligations often take precedence over the fact-and-principle based ethics of the West. To the Chinese, human interests often come before logic-based efficiency and profits.

That said, the Chinese are both intelligent and clever and they know that the West is not going to adopt their way of doing business and that they have to learn to understand and deal with Western ethics on an acceptable level. Business-oriented schools throughout China offer courses on Western style ethics.

At the same time, the Chinese resent Westerners who come to China and attempt to force them to follow Western ethics in their business relationships. This is true even when it is obvious that the Western way would be more beneficial than the Chinese way. And it is also true that there are elements of the traditional Chinese way of doing business that are better than the Western way, which typically gives profit precedence over the interests of both employees and consumers.

In establishing a code of ethics for a new enterprise in China Westerners should work closely with the Chinese side of the operation to create rules that account for the primary interests of both sides. In fact, it can be wise to ask the Chinese side to develop the initial draft of the codes, and then work with them to resolve any significant issues.

China's top leaders have come up with a way of explaining the many changes they have been forced to make to contend with the forces of capitalism, international competition, and the globalism of the world's economies that were not in their original plans. They refer to this factor as *Guo Qing* (Gwoh Cheeng), which translates as "Special National Circumstances"— a clever ploy that allows them to make the changes without officially losing face.

Still, the core value systems of business in China today remain the fundamental philosophies of Confucianism (harmony), Taoism (relationships), and the Tao master and author of *The Art of War*, Sun Tzu (take advantage of the weaknesses of your enemies and attack only when you are assured of victory).

Doing business in China used to be just about cutting manufacturing costs. Today it's more about selling goods and services to Chinese consumers. Whatever form of business you are interested in it is a mistake to be overly impressed or made timid by the historical grandeur of China, the impressive social etiquette that persists, or the philosophical foundations of the Chinese way of doing business.

While there are aspects of the traditional Chinese way that are admirable and should be continued, there are others that are no longer rational or beneficial to anyone. One of the challenges is to discern the difference and make the right choice.

The pitfalls are numerous, and a very sensible recourse is to obtain the services of someone who knows where they are and can guide you around them.

HIGH-TECH BONANZA TAKES A HIT

In 2012 an inspection of the factories in China that assemble iPhones and iPads for Apple and other high-tech American companies revealed that many of the employees worked up to

60 hours a week. The official limit in China is 49 hours per week, but that restriction had generally been ignored.

All of the factories inspected were owned by a Taiwanese company, Hon Hai Precision Industry Co., also known as Foxconn, which at that time employed 1.2 million workers in China. Following the inspection Foxconn announced that it would follow the legal limit. Other notable American companies that were using Foxconn's China factories for assembling their products included Microsoft and Hewlett-Packard.

Apple and other American companies depending on Chinese labor had been notified before about the infringement of China's labor laws but according to labor unions had ignored the warnings. One of the excuses used by a company executive was "Many of the workers are young and single and have nothing better to do and they want to work overtime to make more money." The managers did, however, have emergency exit doors unblocked and the amount of aluminum dust in the air reduced after an explosion killed four workers.

Apple has had a record of inspecting the factories on its own and making significant changes in working hours and safety measures after the media picked up on the story several years ago.

THE CHANGING SOCIAL PERSPECTIVE

That said, another of the key indicators in the new economic and social perspective of the Chinese is their widespread acceptance of shopping on the Internet, something that in earlier times would have been virtually inconceivable.

Alibaba Group Holding Ltd., China's equivalent of Amazon.com, and its *Taobao* [Tah-oh-bah-oh] online shopping site had 2,500 client shops soon after its inauguration, and despite some accusations that as many as 2,300 of its clients swindled overseas consumers by selling them substandard products, and some spats with Yahoo, which owns about 40 percent of the company, Alibaba continued to grow and by 2011 commanded some 85 percent of the online shopping market in China.

Another reassuring factor in Alibaba's survival and growth is that Softbank Corp. of Japan owns some 33 percent of its stock. Softbank is one of the largest and most powerful high-tech-based conglomerates in Japan. In another major step, in June of 2011 Alibaba launched a retail search engine, eTao, which displays shopping sites for people searching for products to buy online. eTao was designed to compete with Baidu, Inc., China's top search engine.

Other online shopping startups like Tencent, Inc. and 360buy.com will no doubt give Alibaba a run for its money. 360buy.com is backed by American investors.

PART TWO

The Historical Perspective

————◦————

Knowledge of the historical perspective of the Chinese, particularly their concept of the cosmic order of things, is essential for an understanding of the Chinese mindset in business, politics, and social matters.

THE YIN & YANG OF THINGS

The basis for traditional Chinese philosophy, religion, science, astrology, and divination is the principle that the universe is composed of and held together by two forces, the yin and the yang, or the positive and the negative, also referred as the principle of duality. In Chinese thought, every aspect and facet of nature is imbued with these two forces, which must be in balance, in harmony, for things to be right with the world—for crops to grow, for people to remain healthy and be content, for governments to function, for companies to prosper, and so on.

In this concept, there is a plus for every minus and it is the interaction of these yin and yang forces that creates life and gives the universe the form and the cycles that we see.

This view of the world, now accepted by most modern-day Western scientists from protons and electrons all the way up, is based on the same yin-yang principle expressed in different terms. It can therefore be said that, to a considerably extent, the Chinese divined the now accepted nature of the universe more than two thousand years ago.

Becoming familiar with the yin-yang principle may seem like a very esoteric pursuit to some Western businesspeople, but recognition of the principle and knowing something about its role in Chinese thought and behavior today can be very helpful in understanding and dealing with the Chinese. It is a factor in what the Chinese eat and in the order in which they eat things— which is about as basic as you can get. It also influences many of the day-to-day decisions the Chinese make in business.

Simply stated, the yin-yang principle gives the Chinese a long-range view of things and allows them to accept the bad with the good as the natural order.

THE PHILOSOPHERS

China is famous for its philosophers, and rightly so. Over the centuries there have been hundreds of them, and they fashioned a body of thought and knowledge that was unsurpassed. The reasons for this extraordinary phenomenon include the long age of civilization in China, a writing system that was developed very early and has remained virtually unchanged down to the present time, and the important role education played in China's ruling class. The work of many of the greatest scholars and thinkers of each generation was thus passed on to succeeding generations.

The best-known of China's sages is Confucius, who taught that harmony was to be achieved by strict adherence to a hierarchical order from the emperor down to peasants and a highly stylized form of etiquette that defined the roles and obligations of each social class. But there were other notable sages who had a fundamental influence on the history of China.

King Wen, founder of the Chou Dynasty and credited with being the father of Chinese religion and industry, was co-author (with his son) of China's most famous book, and is known for his inventions of various tools and technology as well as the creation of the forerunner of calculus. His son, the Duke of Chou, added to King Wen's work. Their commentaries make up the bulk of what came to be known as the now famous *I Ching* or *Book of Changes*. The Duke is also said to have invented the first compass.

Ze Dao is known as the founder of Daoism, which is ranked next to Confucianism and Buddhism in its influence on Chinese thought and behavior. His primary work, the *Dao-te-Ching* (*The Way and the Power*), is said to be the second most frequently quoted work in history (the first being the Bible).

Dao's philosophy was that ultimate reality can be perceived and understood only through mystical insight and cannot be expressed in words. Daoism refers to the way of the universe and all things in the universe—the spirit, the driving power, and the order of all things.

Daoism held that by education, reflection, and intuition, one could achieve harmony in one's personal life as well as with the rest of the cosmos. Philosophical Daoists taught that selflessness and humility were the basis for human conduct, that the ultimate goal of humans was harmony with other people and with the universe, to flow with nature instead of against it and to adapt to it rather than try to change it.

Daoists of this school believed that change was disruptive, that non-action was better than action, that simplicity was preferable to complexity, that informality took precedence over formality, and that the ultimate goal was to conform to the "way" and ride it serenely to eternal bliss. In a Daoist society there would be no classes; all things would be individually or democratically decided; and an all-powerful government would not be needed. It was, therefore, not surprising that Daoism was never embraced by the ruling elite of China, then or now.

THE SEX THEME

Followers of Popular Daoism practiced conventional medicine, science, and alchemy, particularly the search for an elixir of immortality. Later Daoists of this school also preached and practiced an extraordinarily active sex life in order to keep one's life balanced. Sexual relations three or four times a day was considered necessary to ensure good health and long life, and manuals were published giving explicit instructions on a variety of sexual techniques, generally couched in poetic terms.

One of the primary reasons for the growth and influence of Daoism over so many centuries was the teaching that older men should choose young women for their sexual partners, and older women should tryst with younger men. Daoists noted that older men and women would benefit from the energy of their younger partners, while the young men and women would learn from the experience of their older lovers.

THE ROUNDABOUT WAY

A disproportionate number of things accomplished in China are done in a roundabout way, both personal things as well as business. An individual may go through as many as five or six different contacts in order to accomplish one thing. The Chinese keep close track of the favors they do and receive and expect the ones they do to be returned. The foreign businessperson is strongly advised to also use this obligation-building approach to establish a network that can be called upon in time of need.

Another aspect of the problem of getting things done efficiently is simply that the typical Chinese, especially officials, are reluctant to do anything for which there is no established, officially approved procedure. Americans, on the other hand, generally believe it is right to do whatever is necessary to get things done and willingly accept the consequences if there are objections or unforeseen results.

The Chinese attitude is to not do anything (or even to prevent anything from being done) that might be criticized or cause embarrassment or that hasn't been fully approved in advance by everyone who might be concerned. This typical Chinese approach to things is a self-preservation mechanism. With their livelihood (and until modern times their lives as well) on the line, self-defense comes first.

Government agencies traditionally regarded business information as state secrets that were to be protected from the prying eyes and ears of foreign businesspeople at all cost. Part of this, however, was that no single individual had or wanted to take responsibility for dispensing such information—even when they appreciated why someone would need and want it.

There was also in the back of everyone's mind the fear that the government might once again do a flip-flop and make such cooperation with foreigners a serious crime. Significant improvements have been made in this regard in recent years, but it can still be a serious problem.

Over and above bureaucratic inertia combined with the practice of avoiding direct answers, the desire of the Chinese to please foreign visitors habitually results in their giving answers they believe the foreigners want to hear whether or not the answers are true.

This typical Chinese behavior may be innocuous in some instances, but it generally prevents foreigners from obtaining a true or realistic image of what is going on. In business, it can have a highly detrimental effect if foreigners accept what they hear as correct. The only recourse foreigners have is to continue asking roundabout questions and go to other sources.

THE "UNDERSTANDING" TACTIC

One of the fundamental reasons why Westerners often have difficulty in understanding and dealing effectively with the Chinese (and Japanese and other people of the Confucian sphere of Asia) is the widely held stereotype that theirs is a cooperative society and that they live by compromise and consensus. However, the harmony that appears on the surface of life in China—and in the past so deeply impressed many Westerners—is in fact only a surface phenomenon that hides a cauldron of discontent.

The harmony that is seen by outsiders is not the result of voluntary behavior deriving from an enlightened level of goodwill. It is and always has been enforced by all the sanctions available to a despotic government. Those without recourse to a higher or countervailing power generally have no choice but to suppress their dislikes and differences of opinion or to channel them in some other direction.

People in hierarchical societies like China tend to form small groups or factions which then defend their own turf and attempt to force their will on others who are in weaker positions. This is always done with the rationale that the outsider must "understand and accept" their attitudes and behavior as something that is either right or cannot be helped.

This has always been the social structure and psychology of the Chinese and is the source of much of the stress and inefficiency in the country. The natural tendency of each faction is to behave arbitrarily, stretching the limits of its actions as far as possible. When criticized or confronted, these factions and their members either deny wrongdoing in the first place or ask for "understanding" of their situation, which includes accepting or tolerating the situation regardless of what it is.

Social critics in today's China say that the word "understand" is one of the most used and abused words in the language. Parents use it with children, students use it with teachers, trades people use it with their customers, bureaucrats use it with the public—invariably to excuse behavior that is irrational, self-serving at the expense of others, irritating, immoral, damaging, or illegal. Understanding that this system exists does not necessarily mean that one can eliminate it or get around it, but it should help relieve some of the stress in putting up with it.

As those who are intimately familiar with Japan know, the Japanese have also traditionally used this psychological ploy not only in their personal affairs but also as government policy, particularly in their international relations.

China has a serious problem of corruption. Corruption among government officials is said to be especially serious in

Guangdong Province, which adjoins Hong Kong. Graft there is so common that local authorities came up with a special policy of allowing officials to accept a modest amount in "financial incentives" without charges being filed against them. The People's Criminal Investigation Department of the province operates a twenty-four-hour hotline for citizens to report corruption.

Most of the "financial incentives" that go beyond this limit are generally difficult to pin down and prove, and only a very small fraction of them are ever called into question. In the past big league grafters who were caught were subject to being shot.

Bribery remains pervasive throughout Chinese society, but it is generally illegal only when the person receiving the bribe is a government employee. Not only is the person receiving the bribe subject to punishment, so also is the person giving the bribe and any go-between who may be involved.

Trademark counterfeiting in China remains a serious threat to both Chinese and foreign companies, resulting in substantial economic losses. Despite strict laws against trademark counterfeiting, enforcement is complicated by many factors, including conflicts of interest between agencies responsible for enforcing the laws, a hostile environment, especially when foreign companies are concerned, and an almost completely inadequate system of restitution when counterfeiting is proven.

In earlier times the concept of the exclusivity of knowledge was not accepted by Chinese culture.

THE APOLOGY SYNDROME

If there is one thing that will bring out the worst in Chinese authority figures, it is when someone who is known or presumed to be guilty of some offense refuses to acknowledge guilt and apologize.

It has traditionally been the way of Chinese officialdom to deal very harshly with people who resist authority and the idea of being "rehabilitated" (the assumption being, of course, that they are guilty of something), or being punished when the official believes they deserve it.

Part of this old attitude came from the fact that in denying an accusation and resisting punishment, individuals caused inconvenience and trouble for the system. This might result in the government representatives themselves being criticized for failure to keep peace and harmony in their districts.

The key point to keep in mind in any conflict with the law in present-day China is that right or wrong may be circumstantial and based on Chinese interpretations of the situation. Trying to use the logic and epistemology of Western culture to "explain" is likely to get you in deeper.

When foreigners in China get into any kind of trouble, guilty or not, the best thing to do first is to apologize to everybody for causing a disturbance and then get someone else to present your case for you. If you prefer to represent yourself or are questioned, it is very important to remain dispassionate about your *rights* and to take care not to anger anyone. Loud protestations and an apparently uncooperative attitude are likely to be taken as arrogance toward China and its laws and customs.

Doing Business in China

———◦———

It is vital that foreign businesspeople doing business in China be especially sensitive to changes that are going on at all times within the government and in society in general and be both adaptable and imaginative in response to these changes.

For one thing the contract system, under which managers of state-owned enterprises sign contracts with the government to operate the businesses more or less as private enterprises, continues to evolve. As originally applied, the contract management system specified how much revenue in taxes each enterprise would deliver to the government on an annual basis—one idea being that the system would provide more motivation for efficiency and productivity.

Foreign businesspeople must keep in mind that the personal contacts they make are often the only guarantees they have in pursuing business goals, and that these contacts must be continuously nurtured. While the rules of surface protocol are set and fairly strictly observed, there are no specific rules that can be prescribed for dealing with Chinese businesspeople and bureaucrats in every case.

It goes without saying that you should be well informed about your own company and its goals and as knowledgeable as possible about who your counterparts are and what they want. But each situation is usually different enough that it requires its own strategy, devised as you go along. The universal rules that always apply are to be patient and calm, never speak in absolutes or ultimatums, and maintain a cooperative stance.

Given the nature of the Chinese system, success in any endeavor is determined more by individual character, personality, and personal situation than by genuine merit of a project or product, justice, or the common good. For this reason, people on every level automatically think in terms of connections and "going through the back door" when they want to accomplish something.

Probably the advice given most often about doing business in China is the obvious: that to succeed you must learn how to operate within the Chinese system. This includes being patient, using connections, taking advantage of opportunities, and being imaginative and clever.

American businesspeople dealing with China often find themselves at an especially serious disadvantage in taking the "back door," however, since they cannot be as free with gifts and other types of inducements that are customarily used to oil the back-door system. In such circumstances, there is often no choice but to come up with some kind of creative approach that satisfies everybody, which normally requires the help of experienced consultants or go-betweens.

Expatriate businesspeople in China say that before any strategy can be devised for a joint venture it is important to get well enough acquainted with the factory managers and local government officials concerned to find out how each one of them reacts to the possibility of working with a foreign company. It is also important, they say, to find out how effective local managers are in dealing with officials in charge of their area of industry.

DEALING WITH CULTURE SHOCK

Foreigners who have had little or no cross-cultural experience are likely to encounter varying degrees of shock when encountering Chinese culture for the first time, regardless of how friendly the political environment might be. Culture shock comes in a variety of ways and degrees. It can be so subtle that it is not immediately noticeable and is often denied. Or it can be so obvious and shocking that one is completely thrown off balance.

The effects of culture shock are accumulative. Like drops of water on the head (an old form of Chinese torture), the drop may be hardly noticeable at the beginning but as time goes by it begins to sound and feel like the blows of a hammer. It can be the same with little but persistent irritations or setbacks, such as not getting a direct response when you ask a question, being pressed by masses of people, or not being able to take various small services for granted.

Of course, not being able to read or speak Chinese almost always results in some degree of cultural shock for average businesspeople. As far as most situations are concerned, foreign businesspeople who cannot speak or read the language become at least partially illiterate for all practical purposes. They become dependent upon interpreters and the Chinese who speak the language. The cultural differences between China and their own countries are also greatly magnified.

Experiencing culture shock on this level often results in foreigners becoming either antagonistic and excessively critical or, if they want to make a deal, overly eager to please, less critical than they should be, and highly susceptible to pressure from the Chinese side. The Chinese are also masters at putting newcomers under obligation by treating them to effusive, costly hospitality and weakening their position by the use of psychological ploys.

Foreigners with little or no cross-cultural experience tend to interpret Chinese attitudes and behavior in their own cultural terms, even when they know better. It is difficult but vital that foreign businesspeople keep in mind that from the Chinese viewpoint they may be the ones who are off base.

Contrary to appearances veteran China observers frequently note that the Chinese actually feel more compatible with Americans than they do with most other foreign nationalities. They say the Chinese believe that Americans are more trustworthy and respectful than others. It is certainly true that most Americans are impressed by the incredibly long history of China and the arts and crafts of its civilization, and tend to demonstrate this feeling in their behavior. The Chinese like that.

On the personal side, the crowds of people one encounters in the airports, train stations, other public facilities, public events, sidewalks, and in other situations—along with the noise—can be overpowering to the newcomer. There is very little private space outside in the open areas of large cities.

Sanitation in the outlying towns and cities remains a problem that can also be upsetting, and some foreigners find the personal attention they get when out in public in such places eventually becomes irritating.

As in some undeveloped countries, both foreign business people and travelers in outlying regions of China are likely to be approached by touts offering one thing or another, and it is common for outsiders (both Chinese and foreigners) to be over-charged in bars, shops, and other places of business. Newcomers should be especially cautious about buying things from roadside stalls.

THE RACIAL DISCRIMINATION FACTOR

Foreign companies approaching and moving into China often downplay or ignore altogether the personal side of assigning personnel to work in China—factors that include housing, schools, medical care, and so on. This particularly applies to families with small children.

A key point that is almost never considered by foreigners moving to or visiting China is that they cannot just melt into the population and become more or less invisible...like they can in the United States.

The Chinese, Japanese, Koreans, and other Asians who are racially Mongoloid are so conditioned to their racial features—yellowish-brown to white skin, coarse straight black hair, and dark eyes with pronounced epicanthic folds—that they automatically distinguish between themselves and other racial divisions. This means that Caucasian, Black, and Brown foreigners in China are always more or less as "misfits on a stage" who are looked at and treated differently.

For a while this racial discrimination can be a bit of a boost to the ego but it eventually wears thin, and in many people—especially women and children—it becomes a never-ending irritation that can result in serious psychological problems. This factor alone often plays a major role in the number of foreign managers assigned to China who return to their homelands early simply because their wives and children are unhappy.

In outlying areas of China this racial discrimination can be especially difficult for women and children who are blonde, have very light skin, and blue eyes. As the saying goes, they might as well be aliens from another world.

Racial discrimination includes foreigners who were born and raised in China and speak Chinese fluently. They are treated like foreigners who may have just arrived by those who do not know them. Even those who do know them do not treat them the way they do native Chinese. There is always a gap between them. This may not seem like a big deal to people who have never been exposed to such treatment, but it has a deep psychological impact that becomes a burden.

Companies assigning families to China should be aware of this factor and take it into consideration when qualifying managers for their Chinese operations. Some of the more helpful qualifications for family members include liking Chinese food, having an interest in foreign cultures and foreign languages, and being at ease for relatively long periods of time in situations where they cannot read or speak the language concerned. Having an adventurous spirit helps some people but not others; the impact is too personal, too constant.

What this means for most foreign families assigned to China is that they primarily associate with other foreigners in international schools and foreign club enclaves, and behave more or less like tourists when venturing outside of these communities.

For those who are not involved in day-to-day business spending more than a few months in a country as different as China is *not* like taking an extra long vacation in an exotic land.

DEALING WITH GOVERNMENT HURDLES

In many cases the primary problem for foreign companies attempting to go into business in China or expand a business is not inexperience with the culture or lack of knowledge on their part. It is government hurdles they must surmount. These are hurdles created by all levels of government, down to individual cities or towns.

A very important aspect of this factor is that foreign companies and their foreign representatives are characteristically held to higher standards than their Chinese counterparts when it comes to government oversight.

The level of ethical behavior among Chinese companies is generally low by Western standards, and in far too many instances to count Chinese companies stretch the ethical standards set by the government to the breaking point or they ignore them altogether.

Foreign companies that give in to the temptation to take shortcuts, the way so many Chinese companies do, are far more likely to be caught and punished. It is far better for foreign companies to emphasize strict company standards as one of the most important reasons why their Chinese customers, clients, or contacts should favor them.

Once a foreign company in China gets any kind of blemish on its reputation—deserved or not—it is difficult if not impossible to recover it, and the process of trying can be very expensive. Generally, foreign companies cannot depend on their Chinese contacts to help them unless they are absolutely guiltless and the relationship is very important to the Chinese concerned.

POWER CORRUPTS AND SCANDALS PROLIFERATE

There is a fundamental disconnect between many of the principles and policies of the Chinese government and the Chinese people at large. With a little bit of freedom and a lot of prosperity the people want more. But the older generations of government leaders do not want to give up the absolute power they have, and large numbers of their cohorts take advantage of their privileged positions to, as some critics say, "Get by with corruption, lies and murder."

This dilemma puts China's present and future leaders in positions their predecessors did not face—how to maintain control of government policies and not lose public support while allowing the kind and degree of freedom that is necessary for the country to continue its economic growth. So far, the approach that government leaders and those in waiting have taken to deal with this problem is to remain quiet about both present and future policies—a very common traditional practice.

Another basic problem facing China is that the financial system favors the state-owned enterprises that make up a major portion of the country's economic system—a problem inherent in the current form of government.

Financing business growth in China is also filled with pitfalls, and when this is coupled with a heedless obsession for growth the dangers can be life-threatening. Traditionally domestic as well as overseas Chinese depended on personal, private groups of relatives and close friends to raise money needed to start and grow new businesses.

Such personal connections are no longer as common, leaving entrepreneurs dependent upon banks and private loan companies. One notorious example involved a young woman who livcd in Yiwu, a small town near Shanghai, who began as a beautician in her early 20s, quickly established a chain of beauty parlors and hotels and then went into investing in real estate. While still in her 20s she became nationally known as the 6th richest woman in China.

And then things fell apart. In addition to over-spending and not being able to get more money from banks, she borrowed heavily from an underground loan shark who charged a 100 percent interest rate. The interest rates charged by Chinese banks are said to be a little above 20 percent.

The young woman was accused of massive fraud, arrested, tried, and sentenced to death. There was a large-scale public outcry about the severity of the sentence but it was upheld by a second ruling.

The uproar surrounding the case resulted in the Supreme People's Court announcing a number of policy proposals aimed at curtailing the loan shark business, specifically when conducted by civil servants. The Court also ruled that the young woman should be given a second trial because the financial system of the country handicapped entrepreneurs and small enterprises.

The news media suggested that the People's Court announced the new policy proposals and directed that the young woman be given a new trial because in the two years since she had been sentenced to death over 200 small and medium-sized import and export companies in Zhejiang Province alone had gone bankrupt because of the rising value of the Yuan and the cost of labor, and their founder-presidents had absconded to avoid being arrested.

THE CHINESE ADVANTAGE

Generally speaking, the Chinese have a conspicuous advantage in dealing with foreigners. Their skills in both impressing and manipulating foreign visitors have been honed since ancient times. It is a deeply ingrained custom for them to be aggressively hospitable, to give the best impression possible, and to get the most out of their cultural accomplishments, in particular, their ritualized etiquette.

By the same token, when Chinese businesspeople visit the local offices of foreign companies or their head offices abroad, they expect the same degree of hospitality. They are often greatly disappointed when it isn't forthcoming and they are left on their own by their hosts. In the interest of establishing and nurturing good relationships, over and above just being thoughtful hosts, it behooves foreign businesspeople to make their Chinese guests feel welcome and comfortable by fulfilling such expectations.

USING INTERPRETERS

Interpreting on a professional level is one of the most difficult of all arts, particularly when widely diverse cultures are concerned. Interpreting to and from Chinese is said to be one of the most difficult challenges of all, not only because of the extraordinary cultural subtleties of the language but also because of the political connotations of words and the fact that both the vocabulary and nuances of words are changing rapidly.

Since most business and political affairs between China and the rest of the world is conducted through interpreters, it would seem that the profession of interpreter would have high prestige and pay extremely well. Generally speaking, such is not the case. Too many people on both sides continue to regard interpreting as a mechanical function—that converting Chinese to English or some other language and vice-versa is a simple process.

Good interpreters must be both bilingual *and* bicultural to a very high degree. They must be extraordinarily sensitive to myriad nuances of the languages they are using, as well as to the relationship between the two speakers, the political climate, and the personalities (and even the moods) of the speakers. They must be actors in the strongest sense of the word, self-confident and aggressive when the occasion demands.

There have been many recorded cases in which mistakes in cross-cultural interpretation resulted in serious aftermaths. The number of unrecorded cases is probably too large to express in numerical terms.

English is now widely taught in China, and the number of people going on to specialized language training is growing rapidly. More and more Westerners are also taking up the study of Mandarin as a professional skill. But good interpreters are still scarce and mostly underpaid and mistreated. Most Chinese interpreters often have had limited or no experience outside of China, are not familiar with the latest technical vocabulary, and have only a general idea of the business concerned.

Foreign businesspeople using interpreters, whether they are Chinese or foreign, should do everything possible to help them. They should carefully brief them in advance and give them as much written material as possible. They should not overload them with long blocks of comment when speaking and not expect them to go on for more than two hours at a time. If a presentation is to last all day and, especially if it is to go on for several days, more than one interpreter should be engaged. In situations where a great deal of sensitive matter has to be transmitted, it is wise to have a backup interpreter as a monitor.

Obviously having to work through interpreters lengthens the amount of time any business conversation or negotiation takes. Because interpreting generally requires frequent explanations, particularly when dealing with Chinese officials and business managers, a good rule is to allow three times longer than would be expected if only one language was being used. The amount of time needed in any such meeting can be significantly reduced by having most of the points you want to make translated into Chinese in advance and passed out to your Chinese counterparts prior to the meeting.

Another obvious point is that you will be much better served if you have your own interpreter instead of relying on someone provided by the Chinese side. It can be difficult enough without prejudicing your case by using a go-between whose primary interest and loyalty lies with the opposite team.

Foreign businesspeople should also keep in mind that it is a matter of courtesy and professionalism to look at the person being addressed, not at the interpreter (a common failing when people have not been briefed on this kind of protocol or had sufficient experience with it). It goes without saying that businesspeople using interpreters should avoid esoteric references, obtuse vocabulary, and complicated phraseology.

Among the industrialized nations, the United States is probably on the bottom of the totem pole when it comes to the appreciation and training of interpreters, particularly where Asian languages are concerned. The American businessperson who does not want to depend on Chinese counterparts for providing interpreters should begin preparing early.

THE COMPANY-TO-COMPANY WAY

The bureaucratic administrative system in China is set up to deal only with organizations, not with individuals. For the most part, you cannot do things as an individual. You must do them as a representative of your company or organization, and when approaching a government office you must have a letter or other document from your company authorizing you to do whatever it is you are trying to do.

THE JOINT-VENTURE WAY

Westerners who are inexperienced in doing business in China (and elsewhere in Asia) may assume that joint ventures provide the easiest and best way to get into the market. That is often true in the first stages of a relationship but the percentage of joint ventures that come apart within a few years (if not sooner) because of different expectations and cultural perspectives is relatively high. A fundamental factor in this situation is that the Chinese side will generally go into a joint venture only when that is the only opportunity offered to them at that time. They have a deep-seated desire to own and control any operation they are involved in—and if they can't own it they will utilize everything at hand to control it from behind the scenes.

THE CHINESE WAY OF NEGOTIATING

Hong Kong-based attorney/consultant James Gorman notes that Chinese negotiators are famed for their shrewdness; that their representatives in important commercial negotiations are well trained in the art of positioning, posturing, pricing, psychology, and effective use of timing; and they operate from the position of knowing their adversary's strengths and weaknesses well enough to obtain maximum advantage to their side.

Western businesspeople dealing with the Chinese sometimes mistakenly associate the cultural traits generally attributed to the Chinese (subtlety, indirectness, speaking softly, avoiding conflict) with their character and behavior in negotiations.

Westerners would be much better off, Gorman says, to look at negotiating with the Chinese as a sporting event in which the play can get rough, and while each side does its best to win the end result should be something that both sides can live with.

He adds that Chinese business protocol is closer to that of the West than to Japan's, and that the primary difference between Chinese and Western protocol is the Chinese emphasis on rank, maintaining proper hierarchical order, and depending on one individual to act as spokesperson for the group.

For Americans in particular the risks in doing business in China are high. Notes cultural authority Dr. L. Wayne Gertmenian: "You can be certain that there will be innumerable, unforeseen challenges, even when there is an honest effort to learn about and understand China and its people. The unexpected in negotiating with the Chinese is common, and frequently results in failures. Most failures are the result of the ignorance of the foreign side in how the Chinese think and do things."

Make sure you have done your homework before going to China. The Chinese plan meticulously and if you have advised them of your coming well in advance they will likely know your business inside and out.

Generally the primary aim in Chinese negotiations is to get concessions that favor them. Always bear this in mind when formulating your own strategy. One of the most important elements of negotiating with the Chinese is to have wiggle room in your requirements so that you can use a give-and-get approach to reaching an agreement, leaving both sides feeling good. Nobody loses face; both sides gain face.

One strategy Chinese negotiators typically use is to begin negotiations showing humility and deference. This is designed to present an image of vulnerability and weakness. You, the stronger player, will be expected to help them through the process, offering concessions to help them overcome their weaknesses.

Above all, be patient and never show anger or frustration. Practice your best poker face before negotiating with the Chinese. Once they see you are uncomfortable they will exploit the weakness. Decisions will take a long time either because there is a lack of urgency, simultaneous negotiations are taking place with competitors, or because the decision makers are not confident enough.

One challenge facing foreign businesspeople going into a negotiating session with Chinese is to determine the rank of the individual Chinese members, since it is not always obvious from their titles. The best approach is simply to ask the Chinese side in advance to provide you with a list of their negotiators, denoting the rank of each. This advance determination of rank is also important for seating arrangements in any lunch or dinner banquet hosted by the foreign side.

In larger gatherings, the Chinese, just like Westerners, use place cards to designate where individuals are to sit. This is always an option even for smaller groups, but it is important to have the ranking members in the right place, and you may want to confirm this in advance with a lower-ranking member of the Chinese delegation.

Another point to keep in mind is that the Chinese do not like surprises. They should be briefed in advance about the subject to be discussed, and the agenda should be followed as far as possible. If it is not, be prepared for lengthy delays while the Chinese discuss the new points at their convenience.

Where protocol is concerned many foreign businesspeople tend to be intimidated by the rigid ritual of Chinese banquets and business meetings. While it is very helpful for the visitor to know something about Chinese etiquette in advance and therefore feel more at ease in following it, the Chinese are not so ignorant or naïve that they expect all foreigners to be skilled in their manners, and they are tolerant.

The main thing is for foreign visitors to remain polite and cooperate and to demonstrate goodwill by following local customs as well as they can. When you are the guest of Chinese, let them take the lead and direct you. If in doubt in any situation, following Western rules of etiquette that you would exhibit toward a respected and valued guest will do nicely—and you do not have to apologize for "'barbarian (non-Chinese) manners."

Expect Chinese negotiators to question everything, repeatedly, and to come up with cost factors that are well above what you imagined they would be. Also be cautious about accepting anything at face value. Negotiators often report that things are going well when they are not. Factory managers do the same thing. It is important to keep your antenna up and your feelers out.

Be cautious of grand-sounding commitments made by officials, especially if you are asked to spend a lot of up-front money. They have a habit of not fully explaining their projects or goals and have been known to lead enthusiastic foreign investors astray. What you see is often not what you are going to get. Many of the joint ventures that are now operating successfully, and receiving positive publicity, were achieved only after years of painful and costly experiences and often then only after intercession by top Chinese leaders to avoid serious negative publicity.

The Chinese do not resolve issues or make decisions at the negotiating table. These are done after and in between meetings. It is also customary for them to informally and unofficially drop hints and make inquiries outside of the meeting rooms, during breaks, and at night.

The Western method of doing things is the straightforward cause and effect approach. The Chinese method might be called a grid or web approach, involving many other considerations, some of which appear to have little if any relationship with the matter at hand. Their attitudes and behavior are therefore often incomprehensible to the Westerner.

When things are not going well, the Chinese will often deliberately delay the proceedings by using all kinds of tactics, without explanation, rather than admit it isn't working out. If the problems are not eventually resolved, the whole project finally just dwindles and dies.

And here is another problem foreign expatriates often face. As soon as they learn something about the Chinese way and begin to express the Chinese viewpoint to their head office as part of their efforts to explain a situation they are in danger of being accused of going over to the enemy and of no longer properly representing their own company. They are thus confronted with having to deal with cultural gaps in front of them as well as behind them.

Foreign expatriates who are new to China are subject to attacks of feelings that the Chinese are doing everything possible to not only defeat them but to bring themselves down as well. An extraordinary effort, plus support from the home office, family, and friends, is necessary for them to transcend this feeling, see the big picture, and hang in.

In China policy changes are likely to occur overnight, without warning. It is therefore essential that foreign businesspeople keep a very open and flexible mind, and stay light on their feet.

The cross-cultural strain of working with the Chinese cannot be ignored. It can be real and it can serious. And it is accumulative. A lot of little things over a period of time can break the strongest expatriate's back.

In evaluating possible candidates for assignments in China, choosing someone just because they have spent time there can be a costly mistake. Many foreigners who have spent years in China may know a lot of surface things about the country but have no skill at all in cross-cultural communicating and dealing effectively with the Chinese in business matters. In this case, cross-cultural expertise, which may have been obtained in some other country, is the most important qualification.

Despite the Western façade of the Chinese involved in international business there are always elements of the traditional culture that color their behavior when it gets down to actual negotiations. Some of these elements are generally so subtle on the surface that many Westerners who are newcomers to China do not take them seriously—attributing the behavior of the Chinese to casual or minor cultural differences that can be ignored. That is a serious mistake.

Without being aware of these differences and being able to cope with them in a positive way foreigners dealing with the Chinese in business as well as political matters are at a disadvantage. Here are primary elements that foreigners must take into account when negotiating with the Chinese in the order they are most likely to encounter them:

Guanxi (Gwahn-shee) / Personal Connections

Already noted in the business vocabulary of the Chinese, *guanxi* (gwahn-shee) refers to the "social capital" that the Chinese have built up with other people—their friends, relatives, business associates, and local officials who owe them favors. This is in contrast to the Western way of depending on information, institutions, and mutual advantage. It makes doing business in China far more personal than it is in the West.

Zhongjian Ren (Johng-jee-inn Run) / Intermediaries, Go-Betweens

While Western businesspeople tend to automatically trust people they have just met to do what is mutually beneficial and legal, the Chinese tend to automatically be distrustful of strangers and to avoid doing business with them until a fairly prolonged period of getting acquainted and establishing bonds of friendship; or when timing is important, bringing in go-betweens or intermediaries to act as buffers and backups to guarantee relationships. These factors can result in a fundamental difference in both the style and pace of negotiations.

Shehui Dengji (Shur-whee Dong-jee) / Social Status

Confucian ethics and etiquette that call for obedience and deference to one's superiors remains strong in China and must be taken into account in the behavior of Chinese negotiators. This element goes much deeper than the typical Westerner might think and should not be ignored. It influences what subordinates say and do and therefore plays a significant role in the style of negotiations as well as what is accomplished. The give-

and-take casualness that is especially typical of American behavior in meetings is rare in China.

Renji Hexie (Run-jee Huh-shay) / Interpersonal Harmony

One of the most powerful elements in the behavior of the Chinese, in both business and social situations, is the importance
of interpersonal harmony—that is, behavior marked by an
overt attitude of friendliness and goodwill that is designed to
make relationships harmonious. In business situations this social imperative typically masks the true feelings and intentions
of the participants.

Newcomers to China, again especially naïve Americans,
are greatly impressed by this surface harmony, let their guard
down, and become much easier for their Chinese counterparts
to manipulate. The point is foreign negotiators should remain
polite and courteous in their own social behavior but not forget or change their goals without getting something they want
in return.

Zhengti Guannian (Juung-chee Gwahn-nee-inn) / Holistic Thinking

The deepest divide between the Chinese and most Westerners
is often the difference in the way they think. Westerns tend to
think as individuals in straight lines for only short time periods
into the future. The Chinese, on the other hand, have been conditioned for eons to think as groups in circles—in holistic terms.

These differences in the way of thinking obviously have a
fundamental influence on both the present-time behavior of the
Chinese as well as their goals. It has a dramatic impact on the

pace and essence of the Chinese way of negotiating, making things go much slower and take longer than typical of Western behavior. Chinese negotiators typically go from one topic to another without there being a recognizable connection, often without reaching a concrete point or measure.

This standard Chinese behavior both mystifies and frustrates impatient Westerners who typically break things down into individual topics—product, price, quantity, warranty, delivery, etc.—deal with them one at a time and come to fast, specific decisions.

If the foreign side is strong enough to force the Chinese to accept the Western approach in negotiations, Westerners should keep in mind that it will not change either the attitude or behavior of the Chinese in the long run. The best that can be aimed for are compromises by both parties that will keep the relationship going.

Jiejian (Jay-john) / Thrift

Until the 1980s the normal living standard for some 80 percent of all Chinese ranged from varying degrees of subsistence level to periods of starvation that would wipe out hundreds of thousands to millions of them. This reality ingrained in the Chinese a virtual obsession with thrift that has diminished dramatically since capitalism became acceptable in the late 1970s, but remains today a part of the character of the people.

This characteristic is part of the traditional cultural mindset the Chinese bring to negotiations with foreign companies, and they are noted for padding their offers to give themselves as much maneuvering room as possible and haggling over price with great determination.

Foreign negotiators should be aware of this factor from the start and take it into account in advance in establishing their own parameters. Reaching an agreement under these circumstances requires considerable patience and determination to be firm but fair.

Chiku Nailao (Chee-kuu Nie-lough) / Endurance, Relentlessness, or Eating Bitterness and Enduring Labor

Over the ages one of the primary themes in the lives of ordinary Chinese was expressed in the phrase "eating bitterness"—something they had to do to survive. They no longer have to endure such hardships in their daily lives but the concept remains a potent force in workplaces, where working hard for long hours is generally seen as more important than skill or talent.

This attribute applies more to workers in areas outside of such major urban centers as Beijing and Shanghai, particularly in the western provinces, and is therefore a factor that foreign factory managers in these regions must deal with. Working hard is considered honorable and is something anyone can do.

Chengnuo (Chung-nwoh) / Promises

All promises made during negotiations should be taken with a grain of salt, says Dan Harris (Harris & Maure law firm), a consultant on doing business in China. "The people you're talking to may say they have government sales or supplier connections when in fact they don't. Such exaggerations are part of doing business in China. Unless they are followed by concrete demonstration, those who take them seriously do so at their own peril," he adds.

Harris goes on to say that you should have your own set of demands you can insist on and then drop as a show of compromise. "While these demands may not be important to you, they give your potential partner the impression that you have taken a hit when you let them go."

Other points Harris makes: It is important to appear confident, but eagerness to close a deal may embolden the Chinese party by making them think they hold all the bargaining chips. Take your time on decisions.

Make sure you have scheduled enough time to proceed in a leisurely manner. Get some rest before you jump into meetings, especially if you are suffering from jet lag. It is hard enough to focus on the issue at hand in slow, protracted business negotiations. It is near impossible when you are tired from the journey there. Just in case, budget for subsequent visits because you may not get a chance to accomplish everything in your plan. Remember, everything takes longer in China.

Harris also warns that doing business in China means putting your company in an opaque culture that more often than not is shrouded in secrecy and suspicion. Trust and relationships are built over a period of time. He adds that while Westerners generally put a lot of faith in contracts, as far as the Chinese are concerned they are often not worth the paper they are written on without a good relationship between the parties involved.

The fact that the Chinese business culture is fraught with suspicion should be a lesson for every company planning to do business in the country. Companies aiming to enter the Chinese market must remember that laws governing corporate partnerships and joint ventures are weak and unevenly applied, almost always to the disadvantage of the foreign company. Therefore, picking the right Chinese business partner and negotiating the best possible terms are essential to your success.

Harris also cautions that one of the key to success in China is to walk away from bad deals and find good ones. "I know that sounds simple," he says, "but the fact is that many newcomers to China business have trouble spotting the red flags and danger zones that indicate a deal is about to fall apart. The result is that they hang in there and keep negotiating with inappropriate counterparts until they end up with a bad compromise and a disastrous deal."

In brief, the contrasts between the Western way and the Chinese way of negotiating can be summed up as follows:

THE WESTERN WAY / THE CHINESE WAY

Individualistic / Group-Oriented
Members Equal / Superiors & Inferiors
Information Oriented / Relationship Oriented
Focusing on Individual Points / Looking at the Whole Picture
Taking Things in Order / Going in Circles
Emphasizing the Truth / Emphasizing the Way
Emphasis on Speed / Emphasis on Bonding
Informal Behavior / Formal Behavior
Meet Direct with Key Figures / Go through Intermediaries
Make Proposals First / Make Explanations First
Present All Details Upfront / Ask Questions to Reveal Details
Impatient / Patient
Get a Good Deal / Begin a Long-Term Relationship

THE TIME FACTOR

Chinese do not automatically equate the passing of minutes or hours with the loss of money or opportunity. The foreign businessperson who tries to negotiate according to a tight time frame creates a situation that may be intolerable to the Chinese. The larger and more important a project the more likely the Chinese will want to discuss it from every possible angle, and then some.

Experienced Chinese businesspeople and government bureaucrats take full advantage of this factor when dealing with foreigners, often deliberately delaying the proceedings simply to squeeze more concessions out of the foreign side. The only recourse for foreign businesspeople is to control their emotions and frustrations and play the game. But after a calculated interval, foreign businesspeople may have no choice but to let their Chinese counterparts know that it is *not* a life or death issue and that they too have other options and can walk away from the bargaining table.

Referring to the use of war stratagems by Chinese in their negotiations, one old China hand observed that while the negotiators may swear by Sun Tzu's stratagems most of them read his book while in high school and now the only thing they remember is the part about deception being a good tactic.

THE ROLE OF DINING & DRINKING

Inviting someone to be your guest at a meal is one of the strongest expressions one person can make to another—and nowhere is this more so than in China. As in other countries, dining and drinking play significant roles in the Chinese way of getting acquainted with and initiating business with foreigners, and it pays to know something about food and alcohol in their Chinese contexts.

The Yin/Yang Principle in Eating

The Chinese have traditionally been guided in their approach to eating by the ancient principle of *yin* and *yang,* which holds that everything in the universe is either positive or negative, wet or dry, cold or hot, light or dark, male or female, plus or minus, and so on, and that there must be a harmonious balance between these opposing forces if we are to stay right with the cosmos.

Within this thesis, every category of food—meat, fowl, vegetable, fruit, nut, liquid—has its own specific yin or yang character and should be consumed in combinations and quantities that are balanced and are in the order they are best consumed. Yin foods are thin, bland, cooling, and low in calories; yang foods are rich, spicy, warming, and high in calories. Boiling foods makes them yin; deep-frying makes them yang.

Regardless of whether any of these beliefs are true—and there is established scientific evidence to support many of them—Chinese food has long been prepared and consumed with more intelligence and more understanding of nutritional as well as psychological effects than existed in any other culture. Chinese doctors have been using diet to cure many diseases for more than two thousand years. As early as 200 A.D. they were writing learned treatises on the importance of a balanced diet.

Main Styles of Cuisine

There are regional differences in Chinese cuisine that range from the subtle to the flamboyant and overall give it a variety and nuance unmatched by any other cuisine. The most comprehensive and popular of these regional styles of Chinese cuisine are Guangdon (Cantonese), Sichuan, Jiangsu (Beijing), and Shangdong (Shanghai). Each of these regional schools has at least one hundred individual, distinctive dishes, and there are more than one hundred minor "schools" of Chinese cuisine.

Some of the specialties of Beijing cuisine are the famous Beijing (Peking) Duck (the original recipe for which is said to have been 15,000 words long), fried meatballs, noodles, meat buns and dumplings, cold sesame spiced chicken with noodles, paper-thin wheat pancakes stuffed with fried shredded beef and green peppers, casserole of shark's fin with cabbage and soybean curd, and sweet-sour fish.

Cantonese is probably the best known of all Chinese cooking styles because so many people from this region spread around the world during the domestic turmoil of the 1800s and early 1900s. It is characterized by the use of dozens of contrasting sweet/sour or sharp/bland sauces, with similar contrasts in colors and textures.

Oil is used sparingly by Cantonese chefs, and many dishes are parboiled before quick-frying. Half-cooking and steaming to preserve natural flavors is also typical of Cantonese cooking. Overall, Cantonese dishes are mild instead of spicy. Ginger is a popular ingredient, and rice is a mainstay of any Cantonese meal.

Some popular Cantonese choices are sweet and sour pork,[1] abalone in oyster sauce, meat buns, shrimp dumplings, "1,000-

---

1. It has been my experience that you can fairly accurately judge the merits of a Chinese restaurant by its sweet and sour pork. If the sauce is good and the meat is lean, tender, and tasty, chances are all the rest of the food served by the restaurant will be good. But if the "pork" is gristle concealed under batter, no amount of the greatest sauce can transform it into something fit to eat—and chances are the remainder of the dishes on the menu will also be less than meets the eye.

year-old" eggs, braised brisket of beef in sauce, chicken with bamboo shoots in sauce, shark's fin soup with shredded chicken, minced quail with lettuce, and baked prawns with spiced salt and chili.

Drinking & Toasting

Drinking alcoholic beverages has a long and colorful history in China. Beer, wine, and spirits have been produced and used since ancient times, and were often the cause of great controversy. The manufacture, sale, and consumption of wine was prohibited and then repealed 41 times during the 2,400 years between the Chou and Mongol dynasties. In 1127 A.D., a publisher brought out a comprehensive distiller's manual covering all wines and liquors made in the country.

From earliest times, alcoholic drinks were invariably consumed in conjunction with food and at traditional ceremonies, such as marriages. Eventually they also came to be popular as recreational refreshments and for their supposedly simulative qualities. One example of their latter role involved a school of poets who drank to stimulate their creative skills and became known as the "Drunken Dragons." One of the best of these poets, Po Li, was out boating on a lotus pond one night while imbibing. He leaned over to embrace the reflection of the moon in the pond, fell overboard, and drowned.

As in other Asian countries, drinking in China has also long been associated with establishing new personal, political, and business relationships, and in celebrating business and political events. Unlike Japan and Korea, however, where there is very strong pressure for everyone to drink to excess, the Chinese are much more tolerant of light drinking and abstinence.

Some of the common Chinese wines are *Shao-shing, Mao-tai, Ngkapei,* and *Meikweilu. Shao-shing* is a rice wine aged in earthenware jugs to a golden yellow color. Gourmets say it should be at least seven years old and is best when fifteen years old, that it should be served warm, and sipped from small cups. *Maotai,* the famous official drink of the Chinese government, is a potent wine made from sorghum. The alcohol content is 140-150 proof, much higher than that of vodka, giving it a kick that is bionic.

Not all Chinese businesspeople or officials are as immune to its effects as it often seems. Many substitute water or some other colorless liquid for the powerful brew, a ploy that foreign businesspeople should definitely keep in mind.

Meikweilu, literally "Rose Petal Dew," is a liquor named after the morning dew found on rose petals in the district where it originated. *Ngkapei* is a strong, blood-red liqueur that is stored in earthenware bottles and served in small cups.

Probably the most notorious Chinese wine, and one that is occasionally offered to foreign visitors, is *Sam Seh,* which means "Three Snakes," and refers to the fact that at least one snake has been soaking in the wine for at least a year. *Sam seh,* a clear "white" wine, reputedly does wonders for one's general health and stamina.

Reciprocating Chinese drinking and dining hospitality can be expensive. Generally the higher the rank of the banquet guest, the higher the *biao zhem* (head rate) charged by the restaurant. The cost is related to the pomp of the banquet—not to the quality of the food—and is a way of showing respect and appreciation to the guest. If, as host, you prefer to choose the dishes you want served, you must advise the chef well in advance.

Several types of liquor are traditionally served at Chinese banquets for both toasting and drinking while you eat. If you empty your glass somebody is bound to fill it up again, so to limit the amount you drink leave only enough space at the top for a little dab. Generally it is the responsibility of the host and the host's staff—not waiters or servants—to see that the guests' drinking glasses are refilled.

Beer and wine may be sipped, but *maitai* (my-tie), the official drink for toasting at formal banquets, is traditionally downed in a single shot. It is acceptable for you to excuse yourself from drinking alcohol by saying that you have an allergy or simply explaining that you do not drink. In that case it is acceptable to toast with a drink like 7-Up or Sprite.

Banquet Seating Etiquette

There is a precise protocol for everything from the invitations to the seating arrangements. In the case of formal dinners the chief host and main guest sit on opposite sides of the table, facing each other. The chief guest is always seated at the "head" of the room, facing the door; the host with his or her back to the door.

Other guests are seated to the left and right of the host and chief guest in descending order of their rank or importance.

Foreign guests who are not familiar with the Chinese custom of seating should not rush to sit down. They should wait for a member of the host's staff to indicate where they are to be seated.

At formal gatherings, the host will make a brief speech, welcoming the guests and making other suitable comments, and then lead the group in a toast. The chief guest normally responds with a few comments of his own and a toast.

Gan bei (Ghan bay) / "Bottoms up!"

This popular toast generally means what it says: you drink the whole thing in one chug. If you prefer drinking in moderation, just smile and say, *Sui bian* (swee-be-inn) which figuratively but politely means "You do it the way you want to and I'll do it my way (and stay sober)."

In afterhours drinking sessions it is common for some Chinese to simulate being more inebriated than they really are, which may be a ploy to avoid drinking more, as what they really want is to encourage their guests to get tipsy and maybe reveal something about themselves or their company.

Traditionally when a host picked up his chopsticks that was the signal for guests to start eating. Today you may hear something like *Rang de chi* (Rahng derr chee!), "Let's eat!" Or something similar in English.

A typical dinner for special guests will consist of ten or more courses (although Shanghai has tried to reduce the number of dishes by more than half!), beginning with a platter of cold cuts. This means it is important to pace yourself.

The accepted way of indicating that you have had enough is to leave some food on your plate. While declining to taste a dish is not considered a cardinal offense, it is polite to try each dish that is served.

Business banquets usually start at 6:30 P.M. and end at 8:30 P.M. Just as in diplomatic protocol, the host group arrives first. There is usually a period of casual chatting in the reception room when tea may be served before the guests are directed to the adjoining dining room.

The principal host offers a welcoming toast to begin the banquet (or shortly thereafter), and it is customary for the principal guest to reciprocate with his or her own toast. Upon toasting, the formal meal begins. At the conclusion of the banquet, the host will again stand and toast, thanking the guests for attending. It is customary for the principal guest to reciprocate in thanks to the hosts.

As soon as everyone has finished eating and the host and chief guest have made suitable remarks, the group ordinarily breaks up and everyone goes home. The Chinese generally do very little if any socializing after a dinner is over—a custom that Westernized Chinese may ignore.

When the party ends it is customary for the host to accompany the chief guest to the door—and sometimes to his car—and the host may stand and wait until the car drives away.

When You are the Host

When you are the dining host in China your hotel catering staff or the staff of the restaurant you choose will help you decide on the menu. **Biao shun** *(be-ow shune),* literally "per person," refers to the charge you pay per person at a Chinese banquet-style meal; a figure that is normally agreed upon in advance when the meal involves several people and is in the nature of a party.

Some restaurants require that banquet reservations be made two or three days in advance.

THE BUCK NEVER STOPS

One of the more contentious problems that foreign business-people must contend with in China is the reluctance of Chinese bosses to delegate authority, resulting in the staff generally not accepting responsibility and passing the buck. Even when someone has authority, he or she will frequently pass the buck to avoid responsibility.

One of the most common examples of this syndrome is when someone is asked for permission to do something or for approval of something for which there is no well-established precedent. The typical reaction is to refuse the request. No one wants to accept responsibility for having made a decision about something new.

To emphasize the problem of how far buck-passing can go, one Chinese official listed the "travel route" for a simple request in a city office. The request was first put into the form of a written draft and then routed upward to the following: department head, assistant manager, manager, assistant general manager, general manager, a place for receiving documents (in-tray), all departments concerned, all department heads, supervisor, vice-director, director, secretary, and mayor. Once the mayor took action, the document was returned to the sender by the same route.

The overall result of this attitude is that typical Chinese employees will not do anything they have not specifically been told to do by a higher-up. The rationale is that they will not gain anything by doing more than they were told to do even though it turns out to be highly desirable. They will definitely be subject to criticism and possibly even termination if the action is viewed as undesirable for any reason.

The don't-rock-the-boat syndrome also affects the quality of the information that is passed on to top management by employees. Not wanting to upset anyone or create any kind of problem, employees tend to report only positive things and to gloss over negative things or ignore them altogether. The boss is therefore often in some degree of darkness about what is going on in the company. By the same token, managers commonly withhold information from employees individually and as a group to avoid dealing with unpleasant things, to save face, because of lack of information, or to gain whatever credit that may result.

These attitudes limit the overall potential of any group or company. When employees in general are not willing to make suggestions, to do anything more than narrowly defined tasks, or to take any new responsibility, it leaves most of the burden for innovation and growth to the top person.

At the same time, outsiders, particularly foreigners, should beware of giving advice to Chinese managers even when asked for it. It is customary for the Chinese to ask foreigners for suggestions on how they can improve their operation, but this is more flattery than anything else. People asking for advice are probably doing the best they can under the circumstances, are aware at least to some extent of the weaknesses of the operation, and will consider it presumptuous if not rude for a guest to actually tell them how they "should" be running their business.

Rather than sincerely wanting advice from an outsider, the Chinese businessperson may just be behaving in typical Chinese fashion, expecting praise instead of suggestions for improvement.

Maintaining face is another facet of this situation. The Chinese will typically go to extremes to avoid losing face or causing a friend to lose face. This greatly reduces the role of honesty and frankness in personal as well as professional relationships. Both the incompetent employee and incompetent manager may go on presuming they are doing a good job and that everyone is pleased.

Because of the sensitivity of individual Chinese to saving face and to respectful treatment, it is not common for Chinese managers, especially in bureaucratic organizations, to single out high-performance individuals for praise. They are treated very much the same as those doing inferior work. This has a detrimental influence on those with more ability and ambition, and they often lose incentive to do their best.

DEALING WITH CHINESE LAWS

Reading English-language translations of Chinese laws and policies, particularly new ones having to do with economic and business reforms, can be misleading, and foreign businesspeople are advised to approach them with caution. Many of the things that are in the original versions are left out in the translations, and both the nuance and the intent can be quite different.

Veteran expatriate businesspeople in China say many of the business reform laws of the country often turn out to be more of a facade than anything else. The government may enforce them when it is convenient and beneficial or when there is no choice. On other occasions, individuals interpret the laws to suit themselves or ignore them altogether.

New laws or regulations that are promulgated often have riders attached that they are on a trial or test basis for varying periods, sometimes up to ten years. There are apparently several reasons for this approach. One is that there cannot be any guarantees that the laws will work. Probably the most important reason is that new top officials want to put their own stamp on the industry and will not want to be locked into place by laws that cannot be easily changed.

This trial provision is attached to virtually everything new, including many products. If there is a failure, no one can be blamed since it was a "test." The result, of course, is that nothing announced or launched (by the government, in particular) can be regarded as permanent. The effect of this is fundamental distrust in the sincerity, integrity, and motives of the government. It is also one of the prime reasons why it is essential to keep close personal contact with high officials in the government and to stay well informed about their fortunes.

Given this situation, foreign businesspeople in China are often operating in a gray area, where they cannot be sure of their status and have to depend on the goodwill and protection of individuals with political influence.

Another consideration having to do with government officials is the amount and quality of the information they have and release to the public, and how individual officials interpret the information they do release. The amount of information (new rules, laws, and policies) released by the State Council and top ministry officials shrinks each time it is passed to a lower bureaucratic level. Therefore, by the time it gets down to the average businessperson, it is often unclear. The lower the party functionary, the less he tends to know or care about the policies of the party leaders.

There is also a strong tendency for the lower cadre not to totally commit themselves to policies announced by the government because they do not have all of the facts, are not sure that the policies are going to be permanent, and do not want to put themselves out on a limb.

FIRST CONTACT

Foreigners must accommodate themselves to the fact that establishing a personal relationship comes before business in China. The Chinese have traditionally been conditioned to be wary of strangers and not to get involved with them. They still do not make "friends" instantly, as Americans in particular are accustomed to doing—even though their friendly attitude may indicate otherwise.

Their position is that since business is a give-and-take process, and it can be successful in the long run only if there is trust and confidence between the parties, the relationship must be on a personal basis. The more personal contact there is, the more familiar each side is with the other, the more likely that differences can be resolved and that the enterprise will succeed.

Another sign of the personal, often arbitrary, nature of business in China is the fact that demands and prices often vary with the nationality of the foreign businessperson. On the personal as well as the businessperson side, there is often one price structure for Chinese and another for foreigners from different countries.

Establishing a business relationship to sell products in China can be extraordinarily time-consuming and costly. One approach that has worked is to make your company and products known to the "right" Chinese indirectly and encourage them to make the first approach. One of the prime reasons for this is that it is difficult to measure the degree of interest on the Chinese side during the usually long period they take to consider a possible project.

There is also the factor that they see an opportunity to pump a foreign businessperson seeking to do business in China for knowledge as part of their on-the-job training, when they actually may not be serious about the product or project.

TRANSLATING YOUR AGENDA

Make sure that you have a complete agenda of what you propose to discuss translated into Simplified Chinese and sent to the Chinese side well in advance, and take extra copies of the translated agenda with you in case more Chinese show up than what might be expected—a ploy that the Chinese often use in their negotiating strategies.

Be sure to include in this packet the names, photos, and biographical information about each member of your team. This will save you a lot of time in the getting-acquainted process. You should take along extra copies to pass out to appropriate officials and managers not on the mailing list.

Generally, the more of your material you can translate into Chinese the better off you will be from the viewpoint of clear communication and time. When translations are left to the Chinese side you lose a lot of control and it usually takes a long time because the translation sections of the various ministries and organizations are invariably overloaded with work.

SENDING AN ADVANCE PARTY

It is highly recommended that any business mission to China be preceded, by three or four days, by an advance person. This person makes sure that all of the arrangements have been made, including such simple things as confirming hotel reservations and travel itineraries or special preparations, such as audiovisual equipment. Of course, the company with an agent in China can usually delegate this responsibility.

While details such as this frequently slip through the cracks, the Chinese are famous for their personal treatment of official guests. In their wooing of foreign investors they have gone so far as to have special lounges at airports for rent to host organizations for receiving and welcoming their foreign guests. Usually, the welcoming ceremonies at the airport are relatively brief, since the Chinese are genuinely solicitous about the comfort and convenience of guests who often have been en route for many hours.

SHOULD THE CEO GO?

Generally speaking, the chief executive officer of a major foreign company should not go on the first mission to China unless the mission has been invited by an organization headed by someone of equal rank and it has been made clear that the chief executive of the organization will meet the foreign CEO.

The Chinese normally assign negotiating duties to lower-ranking managers and staff members, and bring in the higher or highest executives for the signing of a contract or the opening of a new plant. At the same time, the higher the rank of the foreign mission leader, the more obvious it is to the Chinese that the mission is important to the foreign side and the more likely they are to assign it higher priority. But if it is a first-time visit and there is no "friendship" involved, they cannot be expected to involve the highest officials.

A main point to keep in mind is that once a relationship has been established the Chinese are meticulous about matching rank with rank in their dealings with foreigners. Visitors should not overplay a hand by trying to outrank the other side in any kind of meeting.

It is also unwise to later send a representative for any kind of follow-up who is conspicuously younger and less experienced than the Chinese he or she will be dealing with.

ASPECTS OF BUSINESS MEETINGS

In China punctuality is considered a special virtue. Foreign delegations are normally greeted upon arrival by a representative of the Chinese side and escorted to the meeting room. The Chinese team will normally be on hand when the foreign team arrives.

Business Cards

Learning and using the names and titles of the Chinese team is extremely important, so the first order of business is to exchange name cards. It is vital that you have more than enough cards to go around in case the Chinese team is larger than expected— something that happens regularly because it is a part of the Chinese way of doing business with foreigners. It is also important that your name cards be bilingual, with Chinese on one side and English on the other. Make sure the Chinese translations on the cards have been done by an experienced professional.

Exchanging name cards used to be a carefully prescribed ritual but it is now far more casual. If the situation is very formal, however, it is a good idea to copy the Chinese by using both of your hands to receive a card. In any event, you then look at the card carefully and if there are any questions about the pronunciation of the individual's name, ask them how to pronounce it.

If the Chinese team is fairly large and the introductions go on for several minutes followed by getting-acquainted chats, rather than hold the cards you have received in your hand you can place them in a card-holder, and after you are seated take them out and spread them in front of you. This will make it possible for you to refer to the cards when you want to address an individual, and help you identify who is speaking.

In any case, it is regarded as impolite to immediately put a card you have received into a card case after a quick glance. Stuffing it into a coat or shirt pocket is more of a no-no.

There will be occasions when the Chinese team has not yet sat down at the meeting table so you will be meeting them standing up. In preparation for this ask your escort in advance to first direct you to the ranking member of the Chinese team, then the second in command, then others in the order of their rank if he or she thinks it is appropriate so you can follow the right protocol.

It is also important to keep in mind that one of the most important members of the Chinese team may be in the background, more or less incognito.

Seating Arrangements

The ranking member of the foreign team is usually seated to the right of the ranking member of the Chinese team, who will be facing the door. The host representative who escorted you to the meeting, or another member of the Chinese team, will direct you to the proper seat.

More on Interpreters

One or more interpreters are usually on hand at meetings, even though some members of the Chinese team generally speak English. It is also common for one or more members of the Chinese side to speak English without revealing it to the foreign side.

As mentioned earlier, always speak directly to the individual or individuals you are addressing; not to the interpreter. It is also highly recommended that you have your own interpreter at meetings, and that you have indoctrinated him or her fully on your agenda in advance.

The Small Talk

It is normal to spend the first several minutes engaging in small talk with members of the Chinese team. The foreign team leader should start out by re-introducing each of his team members with personal and professional information about each individual. The more personal some of these comments the better the Chinese like them.

The Big Talk

When the meeting is in China and the foreign team is there to present a project the team naturally makes its presentation first. This gives the Chinese an advantage, so it is wise not to reveal all of your goals and strategy up front. The wisest approach is to reveal your agenda step-by-step, getting the understanding and approval of the Chinese side as each step is presented.

Be prepared for the Chinese to ask for a break following the presentation of each step so they can discuss the matter among themselves. Negotiations normally require several days to complete, with wining and dining the first evening, and one or more times more if the proceedings stretch out.

Do not be surprised if the Chinese side suddenly comes up with something that appears to be a serious obstacle to the project—like some government regulation that you have not heard of. This is a ploy some Chinese negotiators use to get concessions from the foreign side. If this happens the wisest move is say you will give it full consideration and then quietly check with the agency or ministry concerned to see if it is a valid matter. This may require engaging a third party, a consultant, or go-between on the side.

One indication that the Chinese side is seriously considering your proposal is that they may host a second a dinner banquet if the negotiations are drawn out but they believe they are going well.

If the Chinese team announces plans for a second dinner, the foreign side should insist on hosting it to gain face. The foreign side should also host the final celebration if the project is approved.

Some obvious reminders: speak slowly in short, clear sentences; do not appear agitated at any time; do not present any kind of ultimatum; do not put any member of the Chinese team on the spot in any kind of situation that might cause them to lose face; be respectful and courteous at all times.

Talk Metric

Be sure that all of the numerical data in your agenda packet has been converted to metric. The U.S. is essentially the only country in the world that does not use the metric system.

To Smoke or Not to Smoke

A large percentage of Chinese men smoke, and smoking has long been treated as something men do at meetings. Despite the discomfort this may cause non-smokers, experienced old China hands say it is not wise to ask the Chinese not to smoke when they are the host.

At the same time, Chinese businesspeople are generally aware that there are smoking restrictions in many other countries. Those who have lived and worked abroad have experienced these restrictions, and may inquire if their foreign guests prefer non-smoking sessions.

If this occurs the best approach is to suggest "stretch breaks" every two hours or so to accommodate smokers as well as those who need to use the bathroom—something that will not upset the Chinese side because they typically ask for or announce breaks when they need to have a private group discussion about some aspect of the meeting.

AFTER THE CONTRACT IS SIGNED

It is often noted by foreign businesspeople experienced in China that the real negotiating begins after a contract is signed. Most of the problems that do occur result from the fact that government officials and company executives have limited authority and naturally tend to interpret the provisions of contracts from their own cultural, political, and economic viewpoints.

It is especially important that foreign businesspeople who sign contracts in China make careful arrangements for ongoing follow-up. The larger and more important the contract, the more important it is to have your own person, or an agent, on the spot.

However, the Chinese generally do not like to deal with agents. They will often do their best to convince foreign partners to dispense with them, and if they do not they will most likely attempt to circumvent them.

Another factor that the foreign side must keep in mind is that the Chinese side will interpret the contract on the basis of their needs and on changing circumstances. In the latter case it is not because they are inherently unethical but because they are pragmatic, and will not, or may not, follow the provisions of a contract that is no longer practical.

The only sensible recourse is for the foreign side to stay in regular contact with the Chinese side to keep updated on changing circumstances as well as personal feelings.

THE MINISTRY OF SUPERVISION

Another factor in signing contracts in China is the role of the Ministry of Supervision, first established in1949, then cancelled, and then re-established in 1987. Its function is to check all contracts signed with foreign interests for any indications of "corruption"—from failure to provide for compensation within legal limits to undercover arrangements that amount to bribery.

The "Ministry of Honesty in Foreign Contracts" operates offices and bureaus in other ministries, commissions, and administrations that are under the jurisdiction of the State Council, the supreme administrative body of the government. To avoid problems with the Ministry of Supervision, local governments also review contracts signed with foreign enterprises.

According to the U.S.-China Business Council the official overall jurisdiction of the Ministry of Supervision covers the following:

1) Investigating problems of the different departments of the State Council, the people's governments of all provinces, autonomous regions, and municipalities in following and enforcing discipline, laws, and regulations, and decisions and orders of the people's government

2) Handling accusations that state administrative departments, civil servants, and other state administrative personnel have violated administrative disciplines

3) Investigating and handling the behavior of state administrative departments, civil servants, and other state administrative personnel that have violated administrative disciplines

4) Accepting appeals raised by civil servants and other state administrative personnel who do not obey administrative punishment decisions implemented by administrative departments, and other appeals that are supposed to be accepted by the Ministry of Supervision according to laws and regulations.

THE WORKLOAD

Business groups invited to China should be prepared for a full, heavy schedule. The Chinese appreciate evening banquets, brief side trips for sightseeing (usually on Sundays) during business trips, and short rest breaks, but they do their best to get as much as possible out of every encounter.

CHINA'S LABOR LAWS

Dan Harris of ChinaLawBlog.com, which covers Chinese laws applying to business, notes that one of the more bothersome of the ongoing problems facing foreign companies in China is dealing with the labor laws. China's labor contract law applies to all of your China-based employees, foreign or not. China's labor contract law even applies to those foreign employees who have a contract with you saying United States or some other country's laws apply.

What this means, Harris adds, is that in many ways foreign employers are at greater risk from their non-Chinese employees than from their Chinese employees because foreign employees still generally make considerably more than Chinese employees. The congruity between foreign and Chinese employees recently got more conspicuous with China's 2011 enactment of its new Social Insurance Law, which applies equally to Chinese and foreign employees.

The new social insurance system covers pension insurance, unemployment insurance, work-related injury insurance, and maternity insurance.

Harris explains that local governments (provinces and cities) determine the contribution rates for employers and employees. Companies can expect to pay about 40% of an employee's wages in social insurance.

The new law lessens the employer's burden for covering work-related injury costs. The new law also includes penalties against employers that fail to make sufficient or timely insurance contributions. This penalty is set at .05% a day on the outstanding contribution. If the employer fails to pay the penalty, additional fines can be imposed by the local administrative department.

If things get really bad, Harris adds, the local social insurance administrative department has the right to collect outstanding amounts directly from the employer's bank account. The law also requires that each employer register with the local insurance administrative department within 30 days of incorporation and register any employee within 30 days of employment.

DEALING WITH UNWRITTEN RULES

The laws governing foreign operations in China are complicated enough, but there is another factor that can make doing business in China more complicated than it appears to be. This factor is the tendency of Chinese officials to apply "unwritten rules" in their reaction to approaches by foreign companies and in their administration of foreign firms operating in China.

These unwritten rules reflect a variety of influences. Some are based on precedents or other model arrangements. Others derive from special guidelines that legally apply only to the Special Economic Zones, while still others are based on "future" laws or regulations that are being considered.

This approach by the Chinese, particularly where "future laws" are concerned, is not necessarily insidious. For the most part, officials and company managers are simply trying to anticipate what is likely to happen in the future and to structure a relationship that will still be workable when these new laws do come into effect.

One of the major advantages of using the services of a law firm with extensive current experience in China is the fact that they have model contracts for use in negotiating virtually any kind of arrangement. Much of the wording of these contracts has already been approved by the Ministry of Foreign Economic Relations and Trade (MOFERT) and can, therefore, greatly simplify and shorten the process.

In forging a final contract, it is better to stick to your guns and make it as detailed and as specific as possible, not only to avoid future problems but also because it is customary for the Chinese to use past contracts as models for future use. If you agree to one contract without really approving of it, there is a chance it will come back haunt you in the future.

HIRING AND FIRING

Hiring and firing in China is controlled by a variety of laws that are quite different from what exists in the West. Dr. Andy W. Chan, Program Leader in the Department of Management at Hong Kong Polytechnic University, notes that attractive pay packages may be a means of attracting workers in China, but there's more to the question of employment than just a fat pay check.

WRITTEN AGREEMENTS

All job agreements in China must be made in writing, not orally. The latter is not legally binding under the PRC Labor Law. Employment contracts take different forms. A worker may be hired for a fixed-term or on an open-ended arrangement, or on a job by job basis. It is important, therefore, for an employer to state clearly the nature and duration of the contract. Otherwise, it will be assumed by the worker that he or she is on an open-ended contract which is difficult for an employer to rescind.

Workers can be fired for serious misconduct, or in a retrenchment, but they must be paid compensation which is usually one month's pay for every full year of service.

There should also be a probationary period before a worker is taken on staff to enable an employer to decide whether the worker is suitable. In many regions of China, this period cannot exceed one month for a one-year employment contract.

WAGES & WORKING HOURS

China has a minimum wage policy which varies from region to region. It takes into account living standards in the different regions. The law also states that employers should observe a five-day work week, and that an employee shall not work more than 40 hours a week. Overtime is allowed, but in general it is limited to one hour per day. In special cases, three hours per day is permitted. But a worker's total overtime work cannot exceed 36 hours a month.

There are rules on overtime pay as well. On normal working days, overtime pay should not be less than 1.5 times the regular rate; on rest days or statutory holidays, it should not be below twice or thrice the regular rate respectively. China observes ten paid statutory holidays.

Employees are eligible for paid annual leave but no clear regulation has been promulgated. As a result, many firms do not give their staff annual leave as such, but allow them to take six days off a year.

However, there are regulations in many regions that entitle workers to marriage leave, bereavement leave, maternity, recuperation, and other domestic leave.

PENSIONS & MEDICAL PLANS

Both employers and employees must contribute to a workers' pension fund. The employer is required to contribute 20% of a staff's monthly salary, while the employee contributes 8% of his or her monthly pay.

Similar payments are made to medical insurance schemes with employers forking out the larger share. But such contributions vary from region to region. Foreign firms tend to provide more generous medical plans than their local counterparts to attract staff. Both employers and employees also contribute to a national scheme set up to help the jobless.

With China's accession to the WTO, employment regulations are deemed to be revised and changed rapidly. Employers should keep a close eye on the changes.

QUALITY-CONTROL PROBLEMS

China's cultural similarity to Japan often breaks down completely when it comes to quality control by new factories in outlying provinces. Instead of Total Quality Control, to which Japanese dedication verges on obsession, ordinary workers in the provincial areas of China either never think about quality control as anything special or important or look at it as something extra that management is trying to force on them for no justifiable reason.

That said, dramatic advances have been made in the quality of most goods coming out of China. Some are comparable to the things made in South Korea and Japan, but there are still problems, often related to chemicals in the products. One of the factors in quality control in China is that foreign importers and outsourcers often give more priority to cost than they do to the integrity of the materials and the quality of the products.

There are numerous national and local government entities that have varying kinds and degrees of responsibility in ensuring quality control procedures are followed. But it is essential that quality control be a significant element in the relationships foreign companies have in China. It cannot be taken for granted.

As it happens, some foreign importers hide the origin of the products they import from Mainland China by routing the paperwork through a Hong Kong trading company. Hong Kong trading companies are superior to Mainland Chinese companies in virtually every aspect of business—fewer mistakes, less paperwork, faster processing, more accountability, etc.

ARBITRATION IN DISPUTES

As the volume and complexity of Chinese-foreign joint ventures increase, so too do disputes between partners. In the early years, most foreign companies generally took such disputes to the appropriate government offices, often with unhappy results. Now both parties are more likely to take their conflicts to the Foreign Economic and Trade Arbitration Commission (FETAC), an agency of the China Council for the Promotion of International Trade (CCIPT).

Dating from 1952, the Commission saw little action until 1983, when the pace of China's international involvement picked up dramatically. New rules were passed in 1998. The Commission now receives over one hundred disputes a year and has a substantial backlog of cases.

Some 75 percent of the cases brought before the Commission are trade disputes involving the quality of goods or late arrivals and payments. Most of the quality disputes are lodged by the Chinese side, while most of the complaints about late payments are made by the foreign side. Another 15 percent of the disputes concerns such things as insufficient financing, poor management, and arbitrary changes in both workers and management by the Chinese side. Other disputes involve labor and construction contracts, real estate, copyrights, and patents.

The Commission has cooperation contracts with arbitration organizations in several foreign countries, including Japan, Sweden, France, and Italy, and working relations with similar organizations in Hong Kong and Canada.

Disputes between foreign and Chinese companies are inevitable, and should not be taken lightly. While the ethics of Chinese courts have improved considerably since the 1990s they differ significantly from one jurisdiction to the next and with the nature of the dispute. Experienced legal representation is imperative.

Fortunately, the Chinese dislike litigation even more than most Westerners because in the past judges made and enforced laws to suit themselves and their patrons. As result, most disputes are settled through informal meditation, taking whatever time is necessary to work out acceptable compromises between the parties.

MERGERS & ACQUISITIONS

Mergers and acquisitions play a major role in the Chinese economy, and as in most things in China the rules have their own Chinese characteristics, with the government *zou chu guo men* (joe chuu gwoh mun), or "going out of policy," when it deems an M&A will contribute to China's economy.

James C. Chapman, a partner in Foley & Lardner, and attorney Linlin Li, member of the Association for Corporate

Growth, report that the number of M&As has increased dramatically since 2010.

However, they caution that there are often risks foreign companies may not be aware of. In their words, China remains a challenging environment for foreign investors. Cultural, regulatory, due diligence, and legal obstacles make acquisitions in China risky and difficult.

Foreign companies seeking acquisitions in China are usually aware of well-known risks such as questionable business practices, environmental exposure, and the lack of intellectual property protection. Unfortunately, they are often unprepared to handle a wide range of cultural, legal, and organizational differences presented in China. Successful acquirers in China are those that commit the required resources and efforts, and use best-practice strategies to minimize the inherent risks.

In 2010 the Chinese government published a series of regulations aimed at creating a friendlier regulatory environment for M&A activities, strengthening environmental protection, restructuring state-owned enterprises to encourage them to grow into global companies, and encouraging the development of high-tech companies.

It is essential that foreign companies contemplating a merger or acquisition in China be thoroughly familiar with these regulations. The laws cover such things as management control, title to assets, licensing, financial statements, price-earning ratios, tax compliance, etc.

THE FIVE Ps OF INVESTMENT IN CHINA

The success of a foreign investment project in China is invariably determined by how well the investor follows the five "*P*" principles, say Samuel X. Zhang and Jeffrey L. Snyder, attorneys in the Washington, D.C., law firm of Graham and James. After observing both successful and unsuccessful foreign investment projects in China, Zhang and Snyder came up with an investor checklist for venture planning and execution that involves five *P*s: project, partner, pattern, profitability, and protection.

Expounding on their five *"P"* principles in *The China Business Review,* Zhang and Snyder note the following:

1. If the project is compatible with China's planning goals, the chances of it being approved are greatly enhanced, and if it falls into a priority sector of the economy the chances of success are even better.

2. The partner chosen must be authorized to participate in such an investment project; all of the potential partner's strengths and weaknesses must be taken into account, along with whether or not any other official organization has to be involved in the project.

3. The type of investment structure that would be best for the project must be carefully determined.

4. A thorough examination must be made of the project's anticipated market share, what form profits will take, and the various restrictions that apply to the use and repatriation of foreign exchange.

5. The foreign company must determine clearly the type and extent of protection Chinese law affords such an investment, and a process for settling disputes must be worked out in advance.

Zhang and Snyder add that there are many variables in all of these *"P"* areas and that careful planning and implementation are essential no matter how attractive or desirable the project. The greater contribution a project will make to China's advancement, the more support it will get from key officials. For example, a project aimed solely at capturing a share of the domestic market has much less chance of approval than one that would improve China's export picture.

One of the most demanding tasks is choosing the best partner. This means taking the time to examine all personal partners very carefully. Part of this consideration should be the location of the candidates, since incentives, tax benefits, land-use rates, and other factors vary significantly in different areas. Once a candidate is chosen, the negotiation process presents another challenge: it is normal for the Chinese side to include representatives from half a dozen or more different organizations, some of which have no direct relationship with each other but all of which play some role in foreign investments.

The pattern, or structure, of the investment is a critical element, Zhang and Snyder add, and should be determined only after extensive research and expert advice. As for protection, Zhang and Snyder say that the best approach is to make sure that the documentation creating the enterprise and delineating its operation conforms absolutely with Chinese law and is officially approved by every authority with any pertinent jurisdiction, so that in the event of a dispute the foreign side not only will have maximum legal protection but may also be able to accept Chinese arbitration without fear of unfair or illegal treatment.

CUTTING RED TAPE

Government-created red tape may not have been invented in China but it has been honed to perfection over the millennia.

Foreign companies already doing business in China must conform to an array of rules that can be daunting, and are often surmounted only by using strictly Chinese tactics that involve go-betweens and contacts in government agencies and ministries, etc.

For newcomers to China one of the best things they can do in getting ready to go is to consult in depth with their in-country chambers of commerce or consultants who specialize in cutting or dealing with red tape. The challenges are numerous and formidable. Chinese officials often interpret the red tape rules to suit their own personal, local, and regional interests.

All promises by highest-level officials to the contrary, foreign companies and chambers of commerce in China report that with some local and regional exceptions conditions have not improved over the years and in some areas have gotten worse. Shanghai is a conspicuous exception.

In an effort to reassert itself as China's business capital as far back as 1988 Shanghai established the Shanghai Foreign Investment Working Commission to cut red tape and speed up the process of bringing in foreign capital. The commission, which has jurisdiction over any investment worth more than US$5 million, operates under the principle of "one organization, one window, one stamp," as a means of simplifying the investment process.

In addition to reducing the red tape involved in the application and approval process, the Shanghai Commission also provides potential investors with various research and administrative services, including background on the investment climate, finding qualified Chinese partners, and consulting on China's policies and laws. At the same time, the city took several steps to improve its notoriously bad taxi service.

Other cities and regions in China have since taken steps on their own to reduce the red tape involved in doing business, but they remain formidable in many product and service categories and require expert handling.

GETTING A CERTIFICATION MARK

The *China Compulsory Certificate Mark,* commonly known as CCC Mark, is a compulsory safety mark for many products sold on the Chinese market. It became effective on May 1, 2002 as a result of the integration of China's two old compulsory inspection systems.

The new CCC Mark is administered by the CNCA (Certification and Accreditation Administration). The China Quality Certification Center (CQC) is designated by CNCA to process CCC Mark applications and defines the products that require them.

The certification process usually takes 60 to 90 days and includes the following steps:

1. Submission of an application and supporting materials

2. Type Testing. A CNCA-designated test laboratory in China will test product samples

3. Factory Inspection. CQC will send representatives to inspect the manufacturing facilities

4. Evaluation of the results

5. Approval of the CCC Certificate (or failure and retesting)

6. Annual Follow-up Factory Inspections by Chinese officials.

Getting the Right Certification

Obtaining such certification is not always as easy as it may sound. One of the qualifications for an export-oriented certification, for example, is determined by the level of production and exports, while definitions of what is technologically advanced vary.

Maintaining export-oriented certification may also be more difficult than it sounds and involves making all production and export records, as well as pricing records, available to the proper authorities each year. The process of annual renewal can become a trial. Potter notes that while the benefits to foreign companies obtaining either of these preferential statuses are real and worthwhile, obtaining the status and keeping it requires a thorough knowledge of the intent of the Chinese laws and a willingness to work cooperatively with the appropriate supervising authorities.

The Internet offers an impressive number of services that provide both consulting services regarding the CCC Mark as well as direct involvement in obtaining the Mark for clients.

GIFT-GIVING IN BUSINESS

Just as in Japan, gift giving in China has a long history with its own rules based on different social levels and the occasion. Since expensive gifts and gift-giving on a large scale may be construed as bribery it is important that such implications be considered.

Chinese law states clearly that individual gifts from foreigners are not to be accepted, but in actual practice it is illegal only for government officials to accept gifts. The law does not distinguish between a small, inexpensive gift and an expensive one. In the eyes of the law it is the gesture, not the value. However, the law overlooks the giving and receiving of small token gifts.

It is still common for executives of larger companies to give major household appliances and electronic equipment as gifts to top officials and high-ranking company managers, despite the fact that occasionally someone is brought to trial and punished for accepting such beneficence.

In any event, gifts given should suit the individual and the occasion.

Lower-ranking people receive correspondingly less expensive items. Some things that are popular now are elaborate appointment books, pen sets, calculators, colorful calendars, travel books in full color, and subscriptions to well-known magazines like *National Geographic*. Some insiders advise that personal gifts to individuals should be small enough that they can be pocketed and taken home without attracting any attention, and that they should be given discreetly when you are alone with the individual.

IBM (China) is one of the few foreign companies with enough clout to break the circle of gift-giving, limiting it to the two main annual gift-giving occasions—National Day on October 1 and Chinese New Year's in February.

It is frequently noted that people with political power in China do not need money. Officials are in fact paid relatively low salaries, but many manage to live as if they were very affluent. In addition to a variety of real gifts, they receive numerous benefits in kind from people and companies who want their goodwill and their cooperation. These benefits run the gamut from free trips, medical attention, and hard-to-get repair services to entry into prestigious schools for their children.

A leading economic newspaper in Beijing recently ran a cartoon depicting the gift-giving circle that exists in virtually all areas of Chinese life. The drawing showed cakes and liquor being passed around in an unending circle, which included people wanting to travel abroad, people seeking housing, parents wanting their child in a good school, and so on.

The Chinese tradition of presenting gifts to family members and friends during the Lunar New Year has been extended to sending gifts to officials, which poses new challenges to the country's anti-corruption efforts.

The *Procuratorial Daily,* official newspaper of the Supreme People's Procuratorate, recently reported that among the 30 bribery cases investigated by a district procuratorate in Jinan of east China's Shandong Province, bribes during the New Year period totaled 870,000 yuan ($127,000 U.S. dollars).

Peking University professor Zongliang Huang attributed the gift-giving phenomenon to bribers trying to "buy over" officials in a non-obvious way and make it easier if they ask for favors in the future.

"Festival gifts are simply bribes in disguise, although bribers may not ask for favors immediately," Huang told *Xinhua* (Sheen-hwah), the official government newspaper. However, nearly half of the officials who took bribes during the Lunar New Year believed the "gifts" should not be considered bribes, according to the *Procuratorial Daily* report.

A former high-rank official in southwest Chongqing Municipality defended himself at court by saying that the gifts he took for his birthday coincided with Spring Festival celebrations and should not be considered as bribes. He was found to be in possession of antiques, brand-name watches, and an authentic painting worth several million yuan.

China's Criminal Law defines bribes as cash or properties officials take in exchange for asked favors abusing their power. According to the law, bribes worth 5,000 yuan or less could send an official to prison for two years. Those taking gifts worth more than 100,000 yuan could face more than 10 years in jail, or even life imprisonment.

Traditionally, items such as fine wine, tobacco, tea, and brand-name watches would be on officials' gift lists. New gift ideas in recent years have included pre-charged shopping cards and gifts covering officials' private travel costs. Despite repeated warnings by corruption watchdogs gift-giving to government officials remains a significant factor in doing business in China.

One old China hand notes that a Chinese businessman may ask you outright what you would like to have as a gift, and that you should not be shy in responding. He adds, however, that it is an opportunity for you to indicate appreciation for Chinese culture by suggesting some traditional Chinese item, like a handicraft, a scroll, or tea.

Business gifts should be reciprocated. They are seen as debts that must be repaid, and they should be items of some obvious value. If you are too frugal your gift may be seen as an "iron rooster" (getting a good gift out of you is like getting a feather out of an iron rooster).

ECONOMIC CRIMES

Economic crimes in China range from smuggling, bribery, speculation, swindling, diverting foreign exchange, and trademark counterfeiting to tax evasion. Foreign companies operating in China or planning on going into China must be aware of the dangers and take them into account in all of their dealings.

China has no law comparable to the U.S. Fifth Amendment against self-incrimination. Anyone who is questioned about an alleged infraction and does not fully answer every question is regarded as guilty and is subject to punishment. This reflects the ancient Chinese tradition that those who confess are treated leniently, while those who resist are punished severely. Foreign businesspeople called in for questioning must be very careful about their responses and avoid giving officials any indication of being uncooperative.

Government officials have been known to ignore what is legal according to law in favor of what they believe is a better solution. Tax officials have judged that the "legal" avoidance of taxes was wrong and therefore punishable.

In 2011 the Supreme People's Court of China removed 13 offenses from the list of 68 crimes punishable by death. It was the first time the People's Republic of China had reduced the number of crimes subject to the death penalty since the Criminal Law took effect in 1979. The Court also mandated a two-year suspension of execution for condemned criminals if an immediate execution was not deemed necessary.

The 13 crimes were economic-related non-violent offences, including smuggling cultural relics, gold, silver, and other precious metals, and rare animals and their products out of the country; carrying out fraudulent activities with financial bills; carrying out fraudulent activities with letters of credit; the false issuance of exclusive value-added tax invoices to defraud export tax refunds or to offset taxes; the forging or selling of forged exclusive value-added tax invoices; the teaching of crime-committing methods; and robbing ancient cultural ruins.

The Court also planned to introduce a unified guideline for the use of the death sentence. The Supreme People's Court said that the death penalty should only be applied to "a very small number" of criminals who have committed extremely serious crimes.

China has been reforming its death penalty system since an amendment to the Criminal Procedure Law in 2007 made the Supreme People's Court the only authority to have final approval of all death sentences. The Supreme Court has overturned 10 percent of all death sentences nationwide since 2007 when it took back the right of final review from lower courts.

Also in 2011 the Communist Party's Central Committee issued a code of ethics specifying 52 unacceptable practices and warned that violators would be subject to criminal charges and severely disciplined if found guilty. The official news agency *Xinhua* said the 52 practices included accepting cash or financial instruments as gifts, and using influence to benefit spouses, children, or others in employment, stock trading, or business.

The code forbids "meddling in economic activities against relevant regulations with respect to construction projects, land transfer, government purchases, real estate development and operation, mineral resources exploration and utilization, intermediary services, and enterprise restructuring."

Other banned activities include using public funds for personal interests, engaging in insider trading, and spending inappropriate amounts of government funds on the purchase of vehicles, office receptions, recreational activities, and overseas tours.

PUBLIC RELATIONS IN CHINA

American style public relations has found a home in China. The Chinese have an unquenchable thirst for information and are conditioned to put great faith in the printed word and to depend upon third parties, introductions, and connections. They love staged events, such as receptions, openings, and trade shows, which are virtually guaranteed huge press turnouts—all of which contributed to the rapid growth of public relations activity in the New China,

At the same time, leaders in the PR industry say they do not just copy the Western approach. Public relations in China must have some Chinese characteristics in order to succeed in the long run, according to the Beijing PR Society.

One of the splashiest PR successes in the New China was textbook American. Jixin Teng, director of a deficit-ridden chemical plant in Shashi City, Hubei Province, began looking for a new idea to stave off bankruptcy. At a Guangzhou (Canton) trade fair, he met a trader from Hong Kong who was looking for a mainland source of washing powder. In just 28 days, Teng and his research staff came up with a new detergent that had up to four times the strength of ordinary washing powder. They dubbed the new detergent Power 28, and began exporting it to Hong Kong, where it was called "King of Detergents."

Power 28 was a success in Hong Kong but the market was too small to give Teng the volume he needed to make it profitable. He began distributing the detergent in China, simultaneously launching a major advertising campaign, using television, radio, and newspapers. But the product did not take off. Realizing he had to do more to attract attention, Teng put up a 700,000 yuan building on Shashi City's busiest commercial street. He then signed a contract to sponsor the province's struggling soccer team, which was renamed the Hubei Power 28 Soccer Team, and staged the first "Power 28 Soccer Match" at the city stadium.

The sponsorship was a rousing success. The fortunes of both Power 28 and the soccer team shot upward. Sales of Power 28 went from eight thousand to eighty thousand tons in two years, and the soccer team went from nowhere to fourth place in the National Games. Teng then contracted to finance the Shashi Han Opera Troupe and launched a new line of Power cosmetics. The company now has several joint factories in the Special Economic Zones of Hainan and Zhuhai and is expanding into overseas markets.

All this led to an influx of PR businesses, ideas, people, and products that changed China forever. As in any rapidly-evolving sector, there are also challenges as new practices meet tradition. The Chinese offices of global corporations are much bigger buyers of communications expertise than most local companies, some of which still tend to rely on personal relationships with journalists, forged through gifts and entertaining.

Nevertheless, consultants who have grown up with the industry have become experts in balancing creative campaigns with a deep understanding of the unique media environment. By 2011 the Chinese media had more flexibility and editorial control, but the regulation of media outlets by the Propaganda Department of the Central Committee of the Communist Party of China (CPC) can still be a challenge. It is important to keep in mind that the government has tight control over all media outlets, and media are required to cover important government events.

As a result, media relations campaigns need to take the timing of news releases into account to ensure announcements do not clash with major national events. Issues which are still considered sensitive by the government also need to be handled carefully, and it's considered good practice for clients to underscore their commitment to contributing to the local economy and community, and acknowledging local partners.

Another early example of successful media relations in China was a campaign conducted by Weber Shandwick for a consortium of companies. The government had announced changes to the postal system and had issued a notice "suggesting" that this topic should not be covered in the media.

The changes would potentially have a negative effect on the international companies in the consortium, so Weber Shandwick carefully identified journalists and media outlets with a reputation for being more outspoken and who understood the industry, and conducted one-to-one briefings with them.

This careful approach resulted in dozens of outlets running the desired message. The story was also picked up by major Chinese news websites and portals, including the Communist Party mouthpiece, *People's Daily*, ensuring the consortium's voice was heard despite the media challenges.

One of the most common questions about media relations in China is whether public relations professionals pay to secure media coverage. This question stems from clients paying journalists a "transportation allowance," a small stipend to cover the cost of attending a one-on-one interview or media event. In the past paying journalists was common because journalists in China were poorly paid and publications often don't reimburse their journalists' transportation costs. This situation has improved but as in all markets across the world, the public relations industry in China relies heavily on public relations practitioners' relationships with journalists. The concept of "Guanxi"— connections—is deeply rooted in Chinese culture and its influence is everywhere.

Enticing a journalist to attend a media conference is also quite different from other markets. There are so many press briefings in China that consultants are required to get creative with the "trimmings" and in some cases assign themes so that it is over and above the standard. What might be considered a normal press conference in one market is quite different to what is required in China. But there is increasing competition in the Chinese media, and journalists are now becoming more Western in their approach to finding good stories.

It is easy to make the mistake of viewing mainland China as a single market, when in reality the mainland comprises 31 provinces and autonomous regions across a vast territory, each with its own economic characteristics, development levels, and culture. As a result, the focus and approach of public relations activities must be tailored to local interests.

Another challenge in China is that there are still misconceptions as to what PR is all about. Public relations is synonymous with organizing events and entertainment and there is much to be done to change the image of the industry so the brightest university students see PR as a serious career. This starts with agencies such as Weber Shandwick taking every opportunity to demonstrate the effectiveness of PR through partnerships with the top Chinese universities.

Public relations in China can be an enormous challenge because of geography as well as the media, but with all of developments in business and culture, its future is assured.

TEN KEY REMINDERS

Mia Doucet, consultant on doing business in China, speaker, and author of the bestselling book *China in Motion*, notes that when doing business in China, the ability to navigate cross-cultural issues is just as important as the goods and services you bring to the marketplace. She adds that this is true whether your company is just now considering the China market, recently gained its first sale, or has had a presence in China for some time. Here are her 10 reminders for success in China, paraphrased:

1) Never underestimate the importance of connections. You need to deal with Chinese people who have influence. If they feel you are trustworthy enough, and if they can get their network of contacts to trust you, there is a chance you will succeed. But there is no real trust unless you have been accepted into their circle. At first, they don't know if you will be a good partner, so focus on building the relationship before talking business.

2) Protect your intellectual property by using the same approach you would in the West.

3) Never pressure your Chinese contacts for a quick decision. To speed up the decision process it is better to slow down and work your way through your presentation in a logical, step-by-step fashion. Then stand your ground.

4) The negotiation process will be anything but smooth. Your best strategy is to mentality keep your distance. Explain your position in clear, concise, respectful terms, and be prepared to walk away if your terms are not met.

5) Respect face. Never argue or voice a difference of opinion with anyone—even a member of your own team. Never make anyone appear mistaken or ill-informed. Never say "no" directly. That is considered rude.

6) Keep in mind that most Chinese understand less spoken English than what they can say in English. Their smiles

and nods have more to do with saving face than understanding your meaning or agreeing with you. Talk in short sentences, with pauses in between. Listen more than you speak. Find several simple ways to say the same thing. Never ask a question that can be answered with yes. Avoid all slang. Skip humor altogether.

7) Manage the way you present written information. Document everything in writing and in precise detail. Write clearly, using plain English text. Use sketches, charts, and diagrams. Present your ideas in stages.

8) Prepare every step with precision and care. Do not count on your ability to wing it. A lack of preparedness can cause loss of face and trust.

9) Make sure your facts are 100% accurate in every detail, or you will lose credibility. Do not present an idea or theory that has not been fully researched and proven beforehand. If you make a mistake, you will lose trust in the eyes of the Chinese.

10) Make sure everyone on your team knows how to avoid costly gaffes. Most of us are not naturally sensitive to the differences in culture—we have to be taught. The time-honored passive resistance strategies of the Chinese could bring your company to its knees. It makes sense to teach people the cross-cultural factors that have a direct impact on your profits.

PART FOUR

Key Concepts in Chinese Business Practice

———◆◇◆———

All languages are reflections of the emotional, spiritual, and intellectual character of the people who created them, and the older, more structured and more exclusive a society and its language, the more terms it has that are pregnant with cultural nuances that control the attitudes and behavior of the people. Here is a selection of Chinese terms that are especially important not only in doing business in China but in virtually all other activities and relationships as well—some of them briefly mentioned earlier.

GUANXI *(Gwahn-she)*
The Power of Personal Connections

From the dawn of China's ancient civilization the people were controlled by beliefs, customs, and laws that limited their ability to make personal and individual decisions. Virtually every aspect of their lives was prescribed, or was set by precedent, down to where they lived, what they wore, the work they did, the education they received, who they married, and how they interacted with other people.

Over the long millennia of Chinese history this system along with the beliefs and behavior that supported it became the foundation of the Chinese mindset. There was a precise Chinese way of doing everything.

In such a society the old adage "It's not what you know it's who you know" becomes an axiom of life. Another truism in this kind of society is the fact that it is generally not your intelligence, knowledge, ambition, or motivation that determines your success in life. It is the *guanxi* (gwahn-she), the personal connections you have and how clever you are at using them—already mentioned, and invariably the first cultural code word one hears about in doing business in China.

Guanxi is usually translated into English as "connections," but this English term does not do justice to the cultural implications and importance of the word in Chinese society. I explain the concept of *guanxi* by defining it as relationships that are based on mutual dependence.

There is, of course, a certain amount of mutual dependence in all societies but in the American mindset in particular it is generally secondary to a strong sense of individualism and independence. Our mantra is that we take personal responsibility for our actions and our success or failure. Seeking and depending upon connections is not built into our way of life.

That is not the case in China. The essence of Chinese culture, still today, is based on *guanxi*. The foreigner in China who attempts to get by without making and nurturing connections is almost always doomed to failure.

HOU MEN *(Hoe-uu Mun)*
Using the Back Door

In a society in which personal connections play a paramount role in all relationships—business, personal, political, and otherwise—the typical Western way of doing things is often ineffective, and may be considered both arrogant and rude.

In China where historically ordinary people had no inalienable rights to protect them from those in power and where bureaucracy was universal and honed to perfection, expecting something simply because it was "right" and you should get it, and especially "demanding" something or some action, would get the door slammed in your face, or far more serious results.

This situation resulted in the Chinese having to develop a variety of strategies and tactics to get things done—ways that were unofficial but were a key part of the system—like authorities allowing a black market to function because it provided them with advantages of one kind or another.

The most common of these unofficial tactics was using the *hou men* (hoe-uu mane) or "back door"—that is, contacting and making deals with people behind-the-scenes, in private.

Despite political reforms and cultural changes that have made life in China far more rational and practical, the use of *hou men* remains deeply embedded in the culture, and when there is a "back door" most people choose to take it—and if there isn't one they will generally attempt to make one. This is usually one of the first lessons learned by foreigners working in China.

BAO *(Bah-oh)*
"Social Credits" Like Money in the Bank

In societies that originally did not have laws that allowed people to deal with each other in an honest and fair way, relationships of all kinds—business, personal, political, etc.—were based on trade-offs of one kind or another.

This means that people had to first develop personal contacts along with all of the skills that were necessary to accomplish the results they wanted. In China this cultural factor is still very much in evidence and is known as *bao* (bah-oh), which may be translated as "social reciprocity." I also refer to it as "bartering social credits."

Bao, a principle espoused by Confucius, continues to play a significant role in China's business culture, and might be described as the Chinese version of "Do unto others as you would want them to do unto you."

While the principles of *bao* have their roots in rules governing familial relationships, its influence is evident in the business context. *Bao* is about respecting professional relationships and treating people (both superiors and subordinates) with respect. Accordingly, *bao* holds that those who give respect or are generous to others should receive the same treatment in return.

Bao is closely related to the concept of *guanxi* (gwahn-she) in that professional networks and relationships are seen as vital to getting business done in China, with the Chinese frequently relying on the aid of others in return for previous favors.

Despite the fact that the younger generations of Chinese, especially those with international educations, are gradually breaking away from the restraints of *bao* in order to deal more effectively with foreigners, the use of "social credits" continues to play an important role in all aspects of life and work in China.

It is still advisable for foreigners assigned to China to build up *bao* with business contacts and government officials as rapidly and as widely as possible. Just as in the U.S. and elsewhere, one of the primary ways of building up *bao* in China is hosting dinner and drinking parties.

Another way is doing favors for family members of the parties involved in business relationships.

LI *(Lee)*
Etiquette as Morality and Ethics

The Chinese long ago made etiquette a key element in the foundation of their culture and turned the learning and following of stylized manners into a life-long discipline. Both formal and informal behavior was built around specific rituals that symbolized the hierarchical relationships between people.

The rituals of etiquette were not just surface manifestations of good behavior. They embodied the Chinese concept of cosmic order, ethics, morality, and the law, and applied to everyone. Despite the great economic and social gap between the elite of China and the great mass of peasants, their manners and ethics were based on the same philosophical principles, with the same or similar symbols and rituals.

There were so many rituals, and many of them were so complex that on the higher levels of society ritual masters were required to make sure people followed them precisely. Failure to perform a ritual or making a mistake in its performance was a serious matter.

A precise etiquette, as opposed to laws, thus became the basis for the structure and cohesiveness of Chinese society. Viewed from the inside, the logic of the system was impeccable. However, it did not prevent all friction or violence, and in fact was the source of much of the disorder that has traditionally afflicted China because it forced people into unnatural patterns of behavior and made most of them subject to the arbitrary rule of a tiny minority.

Still today, like most other Asians, the Chinese are famous for their politeness and protocol in formal and personal situations. But there have been dramatic changes, particularly among the younger generations and those involved in international business.

When meeting and interacting with foreigners, particularly Westerners, the majority of the people in these categories behave very much like Westerners. Today, rather than obsess over doing things the traditional Chinese way foreigners should simply conform to the best Western standards of politeness.

When meeting people if you can use a bit of Chinese like *Ni hao* (nee how) "Hello," and *Xie-xie* (shay-shay) "Thank you," so much the better.

Many Chinese businesspeople, especially those educated abroad, have adopted Western first names and welcome their use. However, they should not be used in formal sittings that include others who are not close friends. On those occasions it is best to use the family names and titles (if they have one) of the people.

You will meet new people who do not speak English but have nevertheless adopted Western first names for business convenience. It is generally wise not to use first names until you have met the person several times and established a relationship in order to avoid appearing shallow.

To traditional Chinese, the use of first names implies a degree of personal intimacy that can be misleading to both sides. If there is any doubt about what form of address to use, stick to the surname with the appropriate honorific Mr., Ms., or Mrs., or title.

LIJIE *(Iee-jee-eh)*
Rules of Behavior

This term is also often translated as "rites." If all of the rules governing traditional Chinese behavior were put into a book and thoroughly explained, the book would be several thousand pages long. Well before Confucius, who was born in 551 B.C., the Chinese had developed a meticulous system of personal and private behavior that applied to virtually every action of their lives. As the generations passed, Confucian and other scholars equated obedience to this highly systemized behavior with ethics and philosophy and the moral welfare of the nation.

To follow all the rules of behavior was to be upright and moral and guarantee peace and progress in the nation. Strict obedience to traditional behavior has, of course, changed with the times, but it is still of vital importance in everyday life in China. On an official level, however, much of what passes as sincere manners (and ethics) is no more than form, as in two diplomats saying nice things and toasting each other.

HE *(Huh)*
Harmony in an Upside-down World

The concept of *he* (huh) or harmony underlies all of the aspects of China's traditional hierarchy-based culture, and although dramatically weakened in modern times the concept is still a key part of all relationships in China. The foundation of Chinese style harmony was prescribed by the great sage Confucius.

The three main concepts he developed to ensure harmony were (1) benevolence, which was similar to the "Golden Rule" in Western culture: do unto others that which you would have them do unto you; (2) justice in human interactions, which taught the concept of putting the common good before the individual; and (3) etiquette, which covered the stylized manners and protocol that were prescribed for all interpersonal relationships.

YI *(Eee)*
A Sheep & Spear Equals Justice

Yi means justice-righteousness, and there is an interesting twist to these two concepts. The traditional ideogram used to represent *yi* included a radical that means sheep, and the bottom half of the character is the personal pronoun "I."

So how did the combination of "I" and "sheep" become "justice"? According to the Chinese explanation, justice is the power to tame individual aggression, represented by an ideogram that was originally a hand holding a spear, denoting that human beings should be as docile as sheep...or get speared.

In simpler terms, justice and righteousness refer to the original imperial view that people should be like sheep in their obedience to the laws of the land—and these laws were reflected in the etiquette created to preserve the social hierarchy designed by the rulers.

To modern-day Chinese the concept of justice and righteousness is based on maintaining social harmony within the dictates of what is fundamentally right or wrong, notwithstanding the ongoing power of both the traditional culture and the government.

Further, because *yi* requires the promotion of collective welfare to achieve social stability, the Chinese will frequently consider a proposal from the standpoint of how it would affect the whole. This is often at odds with the Western view that may focus on the benefits to particular individuals or classes.

REN *(Run)*
Benevolence as a Selective Virtue

The ideographic version of this word is made up of three characters. The character on the left side consists of the symbol for "man" and the other two characters indicate two people standing side-by-side. The inference is that one of the primary traits that is essential for mankind and all relationships is benevolence. Ren may also be translated as "humanity."

It goes without saying that throughout the traditional and modern-day history of China benevolence was expected of ordinary people but generally did not apply to those in power. However, this is changing. With affluence giving the people more and more power, the government on all levels is being forced to actually practice more and more benevolence.

CENGCI *(Tsung-t'see)*
Hierarchy as the Great Stabilizer

In order to promote societal stability, the Chinese have traditionally stressed the importance of maintaining hierarchical relationships. While hierarchical relationships can take many forms in China, they all tend to center around deference and respect for the dominant figure in the relationship. Some traditional examples of Chinese hierarchical relationship include ruler-subject, husband-wife, parent-child, the elder-younger brother, and friend-friend relationships.

Again, because the structures of such relationships are important to Chinese culture as a whole, they influence how the Chinese behave in all aspects of their lives.

In the business context, Westerners must be aware of and appreciate the high level of respect the government commands in Chinese culture and act accordingly whether or not the officials deserve it and regardless of one's true opinion of them.

Westerners should also be aware of the strict hierarchy observed within the government itself. Decisions are usually top-down and one cannot expect to get much accomplished if the higher levels of government do not approve.

The parent-child relationship has also influenced Chinese business culture. As the parent has authority over a child, a boss exercises the same power over subordinates. This is a particularly important relationship to be aware of when dealing with family-run businesses.

Even if an adult offspring is the person who exercises control over the day-to-day operations of a business, it is likely that his or her father or grandfather will be the one who ultimately has final say over business decisions, no matter what his level of involvement is with the business.

The elder-younger brother relationship has also provided a model for Chinese business relationships. Elders will generally be given more respect and deference than younger individuals—sometimes regardless of the younger person's ability or rank.

Westerns should also be aware of what person in their host delegation is most senior and afford the greatest respect to him. Finally, Chinese businessmen may be uncomfortable dealing with junior Western businesspeople and only want to deal with senior officials from a foreign company. They may even see it as a sign of disrespect if they are scheduled to meet with a low- or mid-level associate.

BI *(Bee)*
Unity the Chinese Way

The fact that many of the greatest feats of mankind (building long canals, constructing great walls, creating thousands of full-sized terra cotta images of warriors to bury with a dead emperor, etc.) were accomplished in China suggests that the Chinese long ago mastered the art of working together harmoniously and cooperatively.

But this image of China can be misleading to Westerners who are not familiar with the details of Chinese history or with the way the Chinese work together.

In reality the Chinese have always been independent-minded and individualistic but they have also always been under the iron fist of rulers who treated them like cattle, forcing them to behave and work in unison to survive.

Chinese philosophers preached about the wisdom of *bi* (bee) or "unity" and the rulers took their preaching to heart, but they used force to compel people to behave the way they wanted them to. And thus the *bi* of China was mostly a mirage.

Now that the heavy boot of the government is gradually being removed from the necks of the Chinese they are exercising various degrees of freewill for the first time in their history, with the result that life in China has become more chaotic than ever before except in times of war.

Most Chinese are now out to get as rich as possible as quickly as possible, resulting in a lot of friction and frustration that alarms the government—and makes the lives of foreigners living and working in China a lot more unpredictable and interesting.

It is therefore important for foreigners in China to be aware of the historical role of Chinese style *bi*, and to use the term in its modern sense in their relationships with Chinese.

BUDAN XIN *(Buu-dahn Sheen)*
Chinese Style Sincerity

In China, as everywhere else in the world, people are very much concerned about sincerity in all of their relationships—because without it one's trust can be misplaced and abused with serious consequences.

But problems often occur in cross-cultural relationships despite the fact that both sides are aware of the importance of sincerity and often harp on it in their presentations to each other.

Friction and frustration often occur between the parties for the simple reason that their cultural understanding of sincerity differs in a fundamental way.

The Chinese commonly use the term *budan xin* (buu-dahn sheen) in their references to sincerity and in their desire to have *budan xin* relationships with their foreign business contacts. This, of course, is always pleasing to the foreigners, and they readily agree that they too want sincerity with their business dealings.

These relationships are seldom without misunderstanding and friction, however, because in its Chinese context *budan xin* means "sincerity plus understanding"—and the catch is that this understanding means that *foreigners are expected to understand the circumstance or position of the Chinese side, and accept it.*

This, of course, puts an entirely different slant on the concept of sincerity that prevails in the West, and it often happens that foreigners dealing with the Chinese must compromise their expectations and behavior to some degree…if they want to do business with them.

BUHE LUOJI DE *(Buu-heh Loo-oh-jee Duh)*
Dealing with Fuzzy Logic

There are three kinds of logic in China: traditional, Communist, and Western—and you have to know which one you are dealing with to understand what is going on.

Until the latter part of the 20th century Chinese in general were not allowed to behave in purely Western style logical ways, despite the fact that they could and did think logically in the Western sense in virtually all matters.

This situation is further complicated in present-day China by the fact that people who have been educated and trained to think and behave logically in Western terms will often behave in the traditional Chinese way by choice or in the Communist way because they have no choice.

The traditional Chinese way of thinking is what I call "fuzzy logic," meaning that it is not the hard two times two equals four kind of thinking or straight-line thinking. It is "holistic" thinking, or thinking in circles.

Since few Westerners are experienced in holistic or circular thinking, Chinese attitudes and behavior are often confusing to them. But fuzzy thinking (the term was actually invented by an American) is often far more powerful than "straight-line" thinking because it is takes in a lot more territory in terms of time, space, and long-term results.

Westerners dealing with the Chinese should prepare themselves by learning how to use fuzzy logic.

NEI-BU *(nay-buu)*
Need to Know Things

This term refers to materials or information that is restricted to those who are on "insiders" of a company office, professional organization, or government agency. The word is used in reference to printed materials or publications that go beyond what is available in the general news media.

In the past there were numerous government-issued materials that were strictly forbidden to foreigners. The number of such materials and their kind has been significantly reduced since the emergence of China as an economic superpower, but this often depends upon the government agency concerned so it can be dangerous to automatically assume that something is public information. It pays to make subtle inquires if there is any doubt.

CHENG *(Chuung)*
The Power of Personal Loyalty

Westerners are, of course, familiar with the concept of personal loyalty and are well aware of how important it can be in their lives. But the Western concept of the importance of personal loyalty pales when compared with that of the Chinese.

Again because the Chinese have never been able to depend upon their governments to detail and defend their rights with laws that applied to everyone, they have been on their own when it comes to avoiding problems, protecting themselves, and surviving in every sense of the word.

This situation has changed considerably in present-day China, but the average Chinese still has to depend upon the personal loyalty of family and friends to a far greater extent than Americans and other Westerners.

The Chinese therefore put great credence in developing and sustaining relationships that are based on strong *cheng* (chuung) ties. This requirement takes up a great deal of the time and energy of the Chinese when both of the parties involved are Chinese.

Interestingly enough, the Chinese can often develop strong *cheng* relationships with foreigners faster than they can with other Chinese because the cultural baggage that comes with Chinese relationships is far heavier.

Some Chinese/foreign relationships between businesspeople have survived time and war and become legendary.

FALU *(Fah-luu)*
Virtue vs. the Law

One of my favorite Confucian quotes is as follows: "Attempting to rule people by laws that require them to act the same leads to resentment and disobedience of the laws and to feel no shame!" Confucius believed that people should behave because of their inherent virtue; not because of manmade laws.

The Imperial rulers of China (as well as the present-day Communist rulers to some extent) apparently took part of this philosophy to heart because most of China's *falu* (fah-luu) or "laws" were not codified or published. It was left up to judges and others to decide on what was legal and not legal.

In present-day China there are many published *falu* but many of them retain some of the essence of Confucius by being worded vaguely—so vaguely in many cases that their purpose cannot be clearly understood. And when most people ignore them, the government sometimes pretends they don't exist; or that they were just a test.

Like the emperors before them, China's Communist leaders know that if the laws are vague and punishments are quick and severe most people will refrain from doing anything that might even seem to be illegal.

Still today the Communist government of China prefers to rule by directives rather than codified and published laws, which often puts foreign businesspeople and others at a disadvantage because they cannot anticipate how the directives are going to be interpreted.

The only practical approach for foreigners is to get the advice and assistance of experienced Chinese—and hope for the best.

KEQI *(Keh-chee)*
The Key to Success in China

If one had to pick a single word as the key to understanding the Chinese in their business and social life, Wei Yao, a member of the Ministry of Foreign Affairs of the People's Republic of China, says it should be *keqi* (kay-chee).

In a booklet called *Communicating with China* (edited by Robert A. Kapp for the *China Council of the Asia Society*, and published by Intercultural Press Inc. of Yarmouth, Maine), Yao says that an understanding of *keqi* and the ability to follow it is one of the main secrets of Chinese character and behavior.

Yao explains that *ke* means "guest" and *qi* means "behavior," but when the compounds are used together to form *keqi* it means a lot more than "behavior of a guest." When used to describe behavior it means polite, courteous, modest, humble, understanding, considerate, well-mannered, and *moral*.

But all of these definitions are naturally in the cultural context of China. Being humble means not only personal humility, which goes far beyond Western practices. It also means down-playing the status of one's family, friends, employer, and so on. Whereas we have a tendency to brag about our accomplishments and those of the people around us, the Chinese go the other way. The importance of *keqi* also indicates how sensitive the Chinese are to any sign of arrogance or haughtiness.

All Chinese are expected to demonstrate *keqi* in all of their actions, and especially toward foreign guests. In fact, says Yao, the Chinese tend to overdo *keqi* and one most often hears the term used in the negative form, asking people not to be too po-lite, too humble, too understanding.

Yao adds that the force of *keqi* has diminished and is con-tinuing to diminish in China as social conditions continue to change, but that it is still discernible in the behavior of all Chi-nese, including overseas Chinese.

There is also a strong tendency for foreigners to overreact to the formalized politeness the Chinese typically extend to them. It makes most foreigners feel somehow inferior and awk-ward, and as a result they often end up being intimidated by the Chinese and behaving in what for them is an unnatural manner. Part of this overreaction, which, of course, is an form of culture shock, is to be less objective, less questioning, less critical than normal.

REN QING *(Ruun cheeng)*
Human Feelings Come First

Ambrose King, a professor in the Sociology Department of the Chinese University of Hong Kong, says that one cannot under-stand Chinese behavior without an understanding of the con-cept and role of *ren quing* or "human feelings" and *mian-zi* or "face." He emphasizes that traditional Chinese values are based on human feelings as opposed to religious principles used in other countries. This respect for the feelings, especially as manifested by "face-work," is expected to hold society together and make it function harmoniously.

In all Chinese relationships human feelings play a vital role, often taking precedence over all other factors. One of the challenges for foreign businesspeople in China is to first determine what these feelings are, and then devise a tactic for taking them into consideration in the process of dealing with employees, business contacts, and government officials.

MIAN-ZI *(Me-inn-jee)*
The Importance of Having "Face"

One of the cardinal principles of Chinese life since ancient times is summed up in the concept of *mian-zi* or "face"—something that China's Communist party tried desperately to eradicate without success during the reign of Zedong Mao (1948-1976).

Mian-zi is a sense of social status; what a person thinks of himself or herself in relation to all other people. It has been described as "social prestige," with the implication that it is something that society bestows upon a person. It is measured in terms of how high one is in society, one's wealth and power.

Mian-zi has been likened to a credit card. The more "face" you have, the more you can "buy" with it. And just like a credit card, *mian-zi* can be overdrawn, and care must be taken to keep one's account balanced.

Most people tend to credit themselves with more face than they actually have (in the eyes of others). The Chinese tend to be exceedingly conscious of any slights to their *mian-zi* and to the possibility of harming another person's face.

The continuous effort to protect one's own *mian-zi* as well as the face of others is referred to as "face-working" and takes up a great deal of the time and energy of every individual. The higher one is on the social ladder, the more acute is the concern with face.

In both personal and business relationships, it is critical to the Chinese that they maintain face and avoid offending the face of others. Failure to preserve the *mian-zi* of others is tantamount to robbing them of their social status and bringing great humiliation on them.

The concept of face is a bit of an abstraction in that it takes many forms and is somewhat hard to concretely define. However, one can view face as a manner of behavior intended to avert conflict, shame, and general unease and promote respect and flattery for others in both social and business situations. The essence of face is that the Chinese expect to be treated according to their social status and position and are sensitive to anything sensed as diminishing their place.

Twentieth century Chinese philosopher Yu-tang Lin very succinctly summed up the traditional Chinese way of getting things done as "favor, face, and fate." By this, he meant getting things done because of obligations that people owe you and doing things for others as favors for which you expect something in return. It also includes doing everything possible to protect your face and the face of family and friends and stoically accepting the natural and manmade vicissitudes of life as things that cannot be avoided. Lin proposed this characterization in the 1930s but it is still valid for many Chinese.

The traditional saying in China is that "A person needs face just as a tree needs bark." Some argue that face along with money and power make up the three most important factors that dictate personal behavior in China.

Because of the fear the Chinese have of losing face or inflicting damage on the face of others they often have difficulty being candid and forthright in their dealings. As a result, the use of intermediaries or third parties in both personal and business dealings is a deeply entrenched custom.

One of the Chinese traits that evolved from the need to protect face is the deeply ingrained habit of being indirect rather than direct in their verbal responses. In meetings they typically ask questions rather than make comments, modify or qualify everything they say, and often just remain silent.

There is no quick and easy way to change this aspect of Chinese behavior, so the challenge is to learn how to work with and around it. Patience, calm persistence, approaching the problem from different angles, and creativity devised on the spot are advised.

There are several different categories of gaining and losing "face" in China. One is losing face when involved in some negative incident that becomes public. The loss of face may be a result of the action being exposed, not the deed itself. Face can be lost as a result of criticism by others. You gain face by not making mistakes; by being praised by others; by demonstrating wisdom; and by demonstrations of goodwill toward others.

GONGWEI *(Goong-way-ee)*
Flattery as a Strategy

There are many words in Chinese that are designed and used

to show respect and deference to the elderly and superiors, to acknowledge social inferiority as well as demonstrate social superiority, to indicate sex and age differences, to account for extended-family relationships, to seek favors, etc. and etc.

This extensive vocabulary is a result of the vital importance that personal relationships have had in China since ancient times—which in turn resulted in people becoming extraordinarily sensitive to and about all of their relationships.

Another result of this situation is the role that *gongwei* (goong-way-ee), or "flattery," has come to play in Chinese life. With both success and survival generally depending on maintaining good relations with others—in the extreme sense—the use of flattery became a national ritual that was raised to a fine art.

The use of *gonwei* is still deeply embedded in the character and personality of the Chinese, and has become one of their most valuable tools in dealing with foreigners. The Chinese learned a long time ago that Westerners—Americans in particular—are especially susceptible to flattery, and they use it with great skill in disarming and manipulating them.

Interestingly, some Westerners now turn the tables on the Chinese and are effusive in their praise of what individual Chinese as well as the Chinese together have achieved. As long as there is no detectable sense of false humility in this behavior it is well received.

YOUYI *(yoh-uu-yee)*
Friendship Comes First

The Chinese believe that a foundation of friendship must be established before parties can engage in business with each other. Unlike in the U.S. and other countries in the West where business is often conducted on a product and price basis with little or no personal involvement, the Chinese do not put business in a separate impersonal category. The key to becoming friends with the Chinese is not at all complicated. All you have to do is be friendly, polite, honest, sincere, and not patronize them.

It is also important to keep in mind that there is a disproportionate number of charlatans in China who specialize in taking advantage of people—other Chinese as well as foreigners.

SHIJIAN *(she-jee-een)*
Time as a Strategy

Despite having invented clocks—for astronomical purposes, not to impose controls on personal behavior—the Chinese never defined or segmented time as was done in the West. The introduction of capitalism into China in the late 1970s was to change this ago-old behavior. However, there are still areas of time that are conceived and used differently by the Chinese.

Chinese who are involved in international business are generally familiar with the Western "time is money" concept. However, they do not automatically relate it to the pace of business, particularly to first meetings and negotiations, before business actually starts.

When foreign businesspeople arrive in China at the end of a long journey, most Chinese do not expect them to immediately rush into business. Their first priority is to get the visitors settled into their hotels and give them an opportunity to rest up. And generally they will politely but firmly reject any attempt by visitors to alter this routine.

Since there often appears to be no set time frame for the length or extent of negotiations, the Chinese typically use that to their advantage in dealing with foreigners.

One tactic that the foreign side can use to help limit negotiation time is to announce up front that, because of economic or other circumstances that cannot be changed, there is a deadline. These circumstances should be explained in detail to avoid any suspicion that the tactic is nothing more than that. Given the Chinese mind-set and business environment, however, any deadline should be reasonably long and flexible enough to prevent it from eliminating the possibility of success.

Another aspect of traditional Chinese behavior that clashes with the Western way is their custom of giving precedence to the form and process of doing things rather than actually doing them. This generally adds to the amount of time it takes to do things and is a habit that is difficult for the Chinese to break.

In an office or factory setting, the only way to work through this problem is to create a well-defined work procedure that can be explained and demonstrated. This is something the Chinese readily understand.

JITI *(Jee-tee)*
Collectivism Still Counts

The Confucian principle of collectivism states that social stability depends to a considerable degree on the co-dependence of and emphasis on the family and work unit. This principle was long ago incorporated in varying degrees into virtually all relationships in China, and remains a factor that is discernible in business even though it is usually described in different terms.

Chinese businesspeople place great importance on the group, and issues tend to be decided in a deliberative manner. While the opinions of seniors have great influence, decisions are often made collectively and reached through a consensus process. During negotiations Westerners should not be surprised if their Chinese counterparts request time to discuss a particular point among themselves before offering a response.

It is also good strategy for Western negotiators to do the same thing, since it sends a signal to the Chinese that they understand and appreciate.

WENHUA YISHI *(Wun-whah eee-shur)*
Cultural Awareness Vital

It goes without saying that being aware of cultural differences and keeping them in mind when dealing with Chinese is of vital importance—a point that especially applies to Americans because we tend to judge everybody else by our own cultural standards.

Americans also generally tend to treat anyone who speaks even a smattering of English as they do other Americans, which is not inherently bad but often results in the communication being less than one hundred percent. It has been shown over and over again that as little as a two or three percent gap in cross-cultural communication can morph into a serious problem over time.

While it is true that the more English a Chinese speaks the more they have learned about the culture of English-speaking people, it is not always safe to assume that they think and behave like native English speakers—especially if they learned their English in China in the Chinese environment.

The cultural content of a language can generally be fully learned—fully absorbed—only by living for several years in the country of the language, with the best results occurring when one is young.

While the really adept linguist who learned a second language as an adult can shift from one culture to another in an instant and perform the cultural role perfectly, the second language and the second culture remain a performance if they did not learn both of them as a child.

But the intelligent person who became bilingual after childhood still has an enormous advantage in being able to utilize both sets of values in cross-cultural situations. Foreign businesspeople dealing with bilingual Chinese who are in this category should keep in mind that although they may understand very well what the foreigner is saying and respond to the foreigner in an appropriate or acceptable manner when they interact with fellow Chinese they must do so within the boundaries of Chinese culture.

This means they must avoid sounding like a foreigner in order to not disconnect with the Chinese side.

Generally speaking, it is not wise to use colloquialisms when engaging in business dialogues with the Chinese—unless you or your Chinese interpreter can include the Chinese equivalent. The same goes for attempts at humor. The Chinese have a great sense of humor but cross-cultural humor often does not compute.

MEIYOU *(May-yohh)*
Saying No without Saying No

The Chinese almost never say "no" outright, and it behooves

foreign businesspeople to use the same tactic of not being blunt—by saying the kind of things the Chinese do: I will look into it; I'm not sure we can do that; I'm not sure if that is right, etc.—when the situation is sensitive and has a way to go.

The Chinese naturally understand this kind of behavior and will normally continue the dialogue if they are serious about establishing a relationship.

SHÌ *(Shur)*
Yes, I Heard You

It is also essential to keep in mind that when the Chinese say "yes" to something it may be a ploy to keep from disappointing you or just as a way to avoid getting involved. In business and political dialogues it can also mean that they heard you; that they are paying attention; not that they agree with you or are making a commitment. It is often essential to pursue the matter in a roundabout way to find out what is actually going on.

Another aspect of Chinese etiquette is that people generally avoid saying exactly what is on their mind in public. In private and in one-on-one situations they can be as clear and as blunt as Americans. If you want to know the truth about something and how you can deal with your Chinese partner or supplier successfully talk to them privately.

ZHENGFU JIECHU *(Juung-fuu jay-chuu)*
Power Plays

Not unlike their Western counterparts, Chinese who want to induce you to do business with or through them will exaggerate the power of their high level government contacts and other things as a matter of course. It is true that such contacts are generally vital in virtually all business affairs in China. The challenge is to discern when references to their contacts are power plays designed to gain some unwarranted advantage.

This often requires a substantial amount of investigation involving individuals and other companies who are intimately familiar with the company concerned, an investment that can help prevent a serious mistake.

PENGYOU *(Pung-yoh-uu)*
Becoming a "Friend" of China

This is one of the most important words in relationships between the Chinese and foreigners. Most Chinese have what often appears to be an obsessive desire to put their relationship with foreigners on a "friendship" basis as rapidly as possible.

It has also been traditional in high-level discussions—particularly diplomatic and political—for the Chinese to formally designate individual foreigners as "Friends of China." This may be an accurate reflection of the individual's attitude and behavior toward China, and it may also be a form of flattery designed to encourage the individual to be friendlier toward China.

DIANYUAN *(Dee-inn-yuu-inn)*
Holding on to Power

One of the more common complaints lodged against many Chinese business managers is their almost paranoid efforts to hold onto *dianyuan* or power, mostly by reluctance to delegate authority. Managers typically insist on approving every action or transaction, no matter how trivial, which results in misuse of their time as well as reduction in efficiency and slows down the process of business. Often, as much time is spent maintaining this system of management as in actually accomplishing work.

One of the reasons for this attitude and approach, say expatriate businesspeople, is what appears to be inability or failure to distinguish degrees of importance in actions or considerations. Something that is very important will habitually get no more attention or concern than something that is of very little importance. Managers often seem to be incapable of viewing the overall picture.

Another aspect of the problem of delegating authority, which must be based on confidence and trust, is the common Chinese practice of giving responsibility to people who have no authority, and vice versa. Probably the primary reason for this dichotomy is that the traditional Chinese social system did not foster trust or confidence in anyone outside of family members who were under absolute control of the father.

This is also the reason why the Chinese traditionally rely on family members and close family friends and tend to form tightly knit family-type organizations in virtually all of their endeavors. Many Chinese companies are run by one powerful father-figure.

A further result of this type of management is that it works against innovation and enthusiasm and makes it difficult or impossible for employees in different sections or departments to cooperate with each other. Not being members of the "immediately family," they are not trusted.

ZONG HANG *(Johng hung)*
Dealing with Your Head Office

As is often the case in China and elsewhere in Asia, the ultimate challenge facing foreign businesspeople in China is not learning how to deal with the Chinese, but the need to continuously educate their home offices to accept the idea that in Asia some things are done differently, and that they must adapt their approach to fit the local circumstances.

This is one of the reasons why it is important for foreign companies to dispatch older more senior managers to China rather than young people just starting out. Another reason, of course, being that the Chinese will give older managers more respect and credence.

COMPANY TITLES

President / Jongchi *(johng-chee)*
Vice President / Fu Jongchi *(fuu johng-chee)*
Director / Jongjen *(johng-jun)*
General Manager / Jong Qingli *(johng-cheeng-lee)*
Manager / Qingli *(cheeng-lee)*
Assistant Manager / Fu Qingli *(fuu cheeng-lee)*
Executive / Officer / Juren *(juu-wren)*

Additional Business Vocabulary

—◄○►—

Accept - Jieshou *(jay-show)*

Act on behalf of someone - Dai *(die)*

Additional charge - Fujiea fei *(fuu-jay-ah fay)*

Advertise for (help wanted) - Zhaopin *(jah-oh-peen)*

Advertisement - Guanggao *(gwang-gow)*

Agency - Daili *(die-lee)*

Agent (company) - Dailishang *(die-lee-shahng)*; person - dailiren *(die-lee-wren)*

Agreement - Xieyi *(shay-eee)*

America - Meizhou *(may-joe)*

Appointment, make one - yue *(yuu-eh)*

Arbitrate - Zhongcai *(joong-t'sai)*

Assign/entrust - Weituo *(way-tuu-oh)*, weipai *(way-pie)*

Assistant Vice Managing Director - Fu Zongjing Li *(fuu zhong-jeeng lee)*

Australia - Aodaliya *(ah-oh-dah-lee-ah)*, Aozhou *(ah-oh-joe)*

Australian dollar - Aodaliya yuan *(yuu-inn)*

Bank - Yinhang *(eeen-hahng)*

Bank of America - Meizhou Yinhang *(may-joe eeen-hahng)*

Banquet - Yanxi *(yahn-she)*

Beer- Pijiu *(pee-juu)*

Beijing (Peking) food - Beijing cai *(bay-jeeng t'sai)*

Book/reserve - Yuding *(yuu-deng)*

Brand - Paihao *(pie-how)*

Brochure, pamphlet, leatlet - Shuomingshu *(shu-oh-meng-shuu)*

Bushel - Pushi'er *(puu-shur-err)*

Business - Yewu *(yay-wuu)*; trade/deal - shengyi *(shung-eee)*

Buy/sell - maimai *(my-my)*; trade/deal-jiaoyi *(jow-eee)*

Business circles - Shang jie *(shahng jee-eh)*

Businessman - Shangren *(shahng-wren)*

Busy season - Wang ji *(wahng jee)*

Buy - Maijin *(my-jeen)*

Buyer - Maifang *(my-gahng)*

Canada - Jianada *(jee-ah-nah-dah)*

Cancel - Quxiao *(chuu-she-ow)*

Cantonese (Guangdong) food - Guangdong cai *(gwahng-dong t'sai)*

Capital (money) - Zijin *(cee-jeen)*

Cash (check) - Duifu *(dwee-fuu)*

Catalog - Mulu *(muu-luu)*

Chain store - Liansuo shangdian *(lee-ahn-suh-oh shahng-dee-inn)*

Charge - Shouxufei *(show-shuu-fay)*

Cheap - Pianyi *(pee-ahn-eee)*

Chemical fertilizer - Hau fei *(how fay)*

Chemicals – Huaxue pin *(whah-shway peen)*

Chicago - Zhijiage *(jee-jah-guh)*

Chinese food - Zhong can *(jhong t'san)*

Claim - Suopei *(suu-ah-pay)*

Collect - Shouhui *(show-whee)*

Commission - Yongjin *(yohng-Jeen)*

Commodity - Shangpin *(shahng-peen)*

Company/Corporation - Gongsi *(gong-suh)*

Compensation - Buchang *(buu-chahng)*

Confirm - Queren *(chu-eh-wren)*

Contact/get in touch with - Lianxi *(lee-ahn-she)*

Content (ingredients) - Hanliang *(hahn-lee-ahng)*

Contract - Hetong *(huh-tong)*

Cooperate - Hezuo *(hay-jwoh)*

Cost - Chengben *(chung-bun)*

Cost, expense - Feiyong *(fay-yong)*

Cost, insurance, freight (CIF) - Dao an jia *(dah-oh ahn-jee-ah)*

Counter offer - Huan pan *(hwahn pahn)*

Countersign - Fu qian *(fuu chi-inn)*

Cubic meter - Li fangmi *(lee-fahng-mee)*

Currency - Huobi *(hwoh-bee)*

Customer - Guke *(guu-kay)*

Customs - Haiguan *(hie-gwahn)*

Customs duty - Guan shui *(gwahn shwee)*

Cut price – Jianjia *(jee-inn- jah)*

Damage – Sunhuai *(soon-hway-ee)*

Date of delivery - Jiaohuo qi *(jow-hwoh chee)*

Deadline - Qixian *(chee-she-inn)*

Deferred payment - Yanqi fukuan *(yahn-chee fuu-kwahn)*

Deliver- Jiaohuo *(jow-hwoh)*

Demand, needs - Xuqiu *(shu-chew)*

Deposit - Cunkuan *(t'suun-kwen)*

Design, pattern - Huase *(hwah-suh)*; huayang *(hwah-yahng)*

Develop - Kaizhan *(kie-jahn)*

Dining room, restaurant - Canting *(t'sahn-teeng)*

Disagreement - Yiyi *(eee-eee)*

Discount - Zhekou *(jay-kow)*

Distributor - Jingxiaoshang *(jeeng-she-ow-shahng)*

District, region - Diqu *(dee-chuu)*

Documents - Dan ju *(dahn-juu)*

Dollar (U.S.) - Meiyuan *(may-yuu-inn)*

Dozen - Da *(dah)*

Draft - Huipiao *(whee-pee-ow)*

Economy - Jingji *(jeeng-jee)*

Electrical equipment - Dian qi *(dee-inn-chee)*

Employee - Renyuan *(wren-yuu-inn)*

England - Yinguo *(eeen-gwah)*

Entertain - Yanqing *(yahn-cheeng)*

Equality/mutual benefit - Ping deng/huhui hulì *(peeng dung / huu-whee, huu-lee)*

Equipment - Shebei *(shay-bay)*

Estimate - Guji *(guu-jee)*

Europe - Ouzhou *(oh-uu-joe)*

Examine, test, inspect - Jianyan *(jee-ahn-yahn)*

Exhibit - Zhanpin *(jahn-peen)*

Expire, fall due - Daoqi *(dah-oh-chee)*

Export - Chukou *(chuu-kow)*

Exporter - Chukou shang *(chuu-kow shahng)*

Feast - Jiuxi *(jew-she)*

Finance - Jinrong *(jeen-rohng)*

Fire, dismiss - Jiegu *(jay-guu)*

Firm offer - Shipan *(she-pahn)*

First class - Diyi liu *(de-ee lew)*

Flexible - Linghuo *(leeng-hwoh)*

Foreign businessman - Wai shang *(wie shahng)*

Foreign capital - Wai zi *(wie cee)*

Foreign trade - Wai mao *(wie mah-oh)*

Franc - Falang *(jah-lahng)*

Free on Board (F.O.B.) - Jiao Huo Tiaojian *(jaow hwah chee-ow-jee-inn)* Freight - Yunfei *(yuun-fay)*

Fuel - Ranliao *(rahn-lee-ow)*

Gallon - Jialun *(jee-ah-loon)*

Give up, call off - Fang qi *(fahng chee)*

Government - Zhengfu *(jung-fuu)*

Gross weight - Mao zhong *(mah-oh jhong)*

Guarantee - Danbao *(dahn-bow)*; baozheng *(bow-juhng)*

Guest house - Bin guan *(bean gwahn)*

Handle, deal in - Jingying *(jeeng-eeng)*

Hardware - Xiao wujin *(she-ow wuu-jeen)*

Hire - Guyong *(guu-yong)*

Hong Kong - Xiang Gang *(she-ahng ghang)*

Hong Kong dollar - Gang yuan *(gahng-yuu-inn)*

Hotel - Fandian *(fahn-dee-inn)*

Import - Yinjin *(een-jeen)*

Imports - Jinkouhou *(jeen-kow-how)*

In bulk - San zhuang *(sahn juu-ahng)*

In common use - Tong yong *(tung-yung)*

Inflexible, rigid - Siban *(she-bahn)*

Inquire - Xun jia *(shune-jah)*

Inquiry (letter) - Xunjia dan *(shune-jah dahn)*

Insurance - Baoxianfei *(bow-she-inn-fay)*

Interest (money) - Lixi *(lee-she)*

International - Guoji *(gwah-jee)*

Invest capital - Chuzi *(chuu-cee)*

Invitation card - Qing tie *(cheeng tee-eh)*

Invite - Yaoqing *(yah-oh-cheeng)*

Invite to dinner - Qingke *(cheeng-kuh)*

Invoice - Fapiao *(fah-pee-ow)*

Iran - Yilang *(yee-lahng)*

Italy - Yidali *(ee-dah-lee)*

Japan - Riben *(ree-ben)*

Japanese yen - Riyuan *(ree-yuu-inn)*

Joint venture - Hezijing ying *(hay-cuh-jeeng eeng)*

Kilogram - Gongjin *(gong-jeen)*

Kind/type - Pinzhong *(peen-johng)*

Label - Shangbiao *(shahng-bow)*

Law - Falu *(fah-luu)*

Letter of credit - Xinyong Zheng *(sheen-yong juhng)*

Letter of guarantee - Baozheng han *(bow-chung hahn)*

Loan - Daikuan *(die-kwan)*

London - Lundun

Los Angeles - Luo Shanji *(low shahn-jee)*

Machine - Jiqi *(jee-chee)*

Mail (post) - Youji *(yow-Jee)*

Manager - Yewuyuan *(yeh-wuu-yuu-inn)*

Manufacture/make - Zhizao *(jee-jow)*

Manufacturer - Changjia *(chahng-jah)*

Market - Shichang *(she-chahng)*

Market price - Shi jia *(she jah)*

Meet - Huijian *(hwee-jee-inn)*

Minimum quantity - Qiding liang *(chee-deeng lee-ahng)*

Model - Xing *(sheeng)*

Name card - Ming pian *(meeng pee-inn)*

Negotiate - Qiatan *(chah-tahn)*

Negotiate payment - Jie hui *(jay whee)*

Net weight - Jingzhong *(jeen-johng)*

New Year's Day - Yuan Dan *(yuu-inn dahn)*

New York - Niu Yue *(new yu-eh)*

Notice, notify - Tongzhi *(tong-jee)*

Order - Ding, dinggou *(deeng, deeng-gow)*

Origin, source - Laiyuan *(lie-yuu-inn)*

Output - Shuchu *(shuu-chuu)*

Packing - Baozhuang *(bow-jwahng)*

Parts - Lingbujian *(leeng-buu-jee-inn)*

Pay - Changfu *(chahng-fuu)*

Pay back - Chang huan *(chahng hwahn)*

Payment by installment - Fenqi fu kuan *(fun-chee fuu kwahn)*

Payment for goods - Huo kuan *(whoh kwahn)*

Permit - Yunxu *(yuun-shu)*

Place an order - Ding hou *(deeng whoh)*

Plan - Jihua *(jee-whah)*

Policy - Zhengce *(juhng-t'suh)*

Pound - Bang *(bahng)*

Port - Kouan *(kow-inn)*

Price - Jiage *(jah-guh)*

Price list - Jiamu dan *(jah-muu-dahn)*

Principle - Yuanze *(yuu-inn-juh)*

Private (not government) - Siren *(suh-wren)*

Produce - Chuchan *(chuu-chahn)*

Product - Chanpin *(chahn-peen)*

Profit margin - Lirun'e *(lee-ruun'uh)*

Quality - Zhiliang *(jee-lee-ahng);* zhidi *(cee-dee)*

Quantity - Shuliang *(shuu-lee-ahng)*

Quota - Ding'e *(ding-uh)*

Quote, offer - Bao *(bow)*

Retailer - Lingshoushang - *(leng-sho-uu-shahng)*

Revoke - Chexiao *(chuh-she-ah-oh)*

Russia - Ewenguo *(uh-wren-gwah)*

Sales confirmation - Xiaoshou querenshu *(she-ah-oh-sho-uu chuh-wren-shuu)*

Sample - Huoyang *(whoh-yahng)*

Sample book - Yang ben *(yahng bun)*

Seasonal - Jijiexing *(jee-jay-sheeng)*

Sell - Xiaoshou *(she-ah-oh-show)*

Service charge - Shouxu fei *(show-shu-fay)*

Service desk - fuwu tai *(fuu-wuu tie)*

Settle accounts - Jie suan *(jay swan)*

Shanghai (Shandong) food - Shandong cai *(shahng-dong t'sai)*

Ship (send) - Zhuangyun *(jwahng-yuun)*

Shortage - Duanshao *(dwahn-shah-oh)*

Sight - Jiqi *(jee-chee)*, sight draft - jiqi piao *(jee-chee pow)*

Sign - Qian *(chee-inn)*; qianshu *(chee-inn-shuu)*; qianzi *(chee-inn-jee)*

Sign one's name - Qian ming *(chee-inn meeng)*

Singapore - Xinjiapo *(sheen-jah-poe)*

Size - Chicun *(chee-t'sune)*

Slack season - Danji *(dahn-jee)*

Spain- Xibanya *(she-bahn-yah)*

Spare parts - Beijian *(bay-jee-inn)*

Specifications - Guige *(gwee-guh)*

Specified packing - Zhiding baozhuang *(jee-deeng bow-chung)*

Square meter - Ping fangmi *(peeng fahng-mee)*

Square yard - Ping fangma *(peeng fahng-mah)*

Staff member - Zhi yuan *(jee yuu-inn)*

Standard (quality) - Biaozhun *(bow-june)*

Sum of money - Bi *(bee)*

Superior (quality) - Shangdeng *(shahng-dung)*

Supplier - Gongxiao-shang *(gong-she-ow-shahng)*

Sweden - Ruidian *(ruu-ee-dee-inn)*

System - Xitong *(she-tong)*

Television - Dianshiji *(dee-inn-she-jee)*

Terms - Tiaokuan *(tao-kwan)*

Ton - Dun *(dune)*

Trade - Maoyi *(mah-oh-eee)*

Trade show - Jiaoyi hui *(jah-oh-ee whee)*

Unit price - Dan jia *(dahn jee-ah)*

Value - Jiazhi *(jee-ah-juuh)*

Valid -Youxiao *(yoh-she-ow)*

Volume of business - Chengjiao liang *(chung-jee-ow lee-ahng)*

Western food - Xi can *(she t'san)*

Wholesale - Pifa *(pee-fah)*

PART SIX

Glossary of Useful Terms

Airen *(aye-wren)* – Literally, loved one. The term for wife.

Bai-jiu *(by-juu)* – A powerful alcoholic drink that has a strong, burning taste, which foreigners often compare to homemade moonshine or "white lightning."

Bailandi *(by-lahn-dee)* – The Chinese pronunciation of brandy; a popular gift item.

Bang *(bahng)* / Faction or gang. Given China's social philosophy, people are invariably divided into groups and are primarily identified by the group they belong to. In the case of politics, these groups or *bang* are referred to as factions or gangs.

Bao che *(bah-oh-chay)* – This refers to the practice of hiring a taxi by the hour or day and paying a flat fee. It can be very helpful when you have several places to go on the same day when the weather is bad or when you have to go to locations where finding taxis for the return trip might be difficult or impossible.

Bao-xiao *(bah-oh-she-ow)* – China's system of putting work-related expenditures on the office or company expense account is known as *bao-xiao*. The system also includes the use of any personal equipment or accessory that one uses in conjunction with work. The system is apparently going out of date.

Big Road; Little Road – Big Road refers to China's major news media, which tend to reflect the attitudes and line of the government and to be dry and hard to digest. *Little Road* refers to the smaller, unofficial publications that carry popular news, including gossip.

Bu fang-bian *(buu fahng-bee-inn)* – "It's not convenient," a stock expression used especially by bureaucrats when asked a question or asked to do something. It is an institutionalized way of saying "no" without coming right out and saying it. Another version is Bu quing-chu *(buu-cheeng chuu)*—"I don't quite understand" or "I'm not too clear about it," which is used in the same manner.

Bu gongkai *(buu gong-kie)* – "Not open," referring to all places and things "closed" to outsiders, including areas involved with national security and political thinking.

Chadian *(chah dee-inn)* – Teahouse, more commonly called *chaguan* (chah-gwahn) in the North. One of the great public institutions of China for centuries, teahouses fell victim to revolutionary madness in the 1960s, but have since reappeared in growing numbers.

Chi ku *(chee-kuu)* – An old phrase meaning to "eat bitterness," in reference to the extraordinary hardships forced onto the Chinese by their governments and by nature over the centuries. Literally the term means to eat vinegar, and nowadays refers to jealousy, especially the jealousy the Chinese feel toward people who are economically better off than they.

Chu Kuo Tequ *(chuu kwoh tay-chu)* – Special Export Zone (SEZ). Now often called Jingi Te Ou *(Jeen-ghee Tay Oh-uu)* or Special Economic Zones, or just Tequ *(Tay-chuu)*, Special Zone. These are special zones designated by the Chinese government as approved locations for foreign factories, and engaging in the import and export trade.

Dengji *(dung-iee)* – Registration system. As part of China's internal security system, records are supposed to be kept of all visits by Chinese to the offices and homes of foreigners. In the early years, this system was rigorously enforced, with assigned "watchers" recording every move foreigners made and reporting every visitor they had. Enforcement slacked off rapidly in the late 1980s, and is now generally ignored.

Duibuqi *(du-we-buu-chee)* – I'm sorry ("face you not").

Dui wai yinxiang *(du-we wye eeen-shee-ahng)* – The outside world; a term that is pregnant with meaning in distinguishing between China and other countries.

Ganbu *(gahn-buu)* – This word is frequently translated as cadre, and sometimes as official. It may refer to any level of government employee, from a clerk to the top political leader of the country. There are twenty-four grades of cadre, with the lowest being grade twenty-four and the highest number one. Generally, the ranks of individuals are not mentioned in references to them.

Gu dong dian *(guu dong dee-in)* – Antique shop, a favorite shopping place for visitors in China.

Gwei Lo *(gway low)* – Foreign devil, a term used in China for many centuries in reference to foreigners.

Hai shen *(hie shuun)* – Sea slugs. Considered a great delicacy by the Chinese, sea slugs are often offered to foreign guests as something very special (also, it seems, sometimes in the nature of a test, to see how deeply committed an individual is to China).

Hukou *(huu-kow)* – Household Registration Certificate. This is the I.D. certificate that Chinese must carry. It allows the Chinese authorities to keep track of everyone in the country, to control their movements and actions. To *cha hukou* is to check their I.D., often done by officials to harass people. Colloquially when people are over-inquisitive, a Chinese may sarcastically ask: "*Cha hukou?*" (What are you doing?)

Jishu jiaoliu *(jee-shuu jee-ow-lee-uu)* – Technical exchange. This is the term the Chinese use to describe a presentation made by foreign interests wanting to introduce their technology into China. The Chinese may take the position that they should get all of the technology during the presentation, whether or not they intend to sign any kind of contract with the company making the presentation.

Joss (joss) – One of the most used words in Chinese, *Joss* means "luck," something the people previously had to depend upon to an extraordinary degree, not only in respect to the vagaries of nature but also in their everyday affairs, since their rights were subject to arbitrary interpretation by anyone superior to them.

Kai-fang *(kie-fahng)* – Open Door policy, introduced by then Vice-Premier Xiaoping Deng in 1978.

Kai-shui *(kie-shwee)* – Boiled water. Since public water purification systems are rare in some parts of China, it is important that visitors who do not have access to treated water drink only boiled water (or bottled drinks).

Kaolu *(kow-luu)* – "I'll / we'll consider it." A very common expression used to put someone off, to delay something, or to avoid making any kind of commitment; sometimes because the individual approached does not have the authority to respond and must consult with other members of his or her unit; and sometimes because the individual simply doesn't want to be bothered.

Kao-shi *(kow-shee)* – Examinations. Although exams in China are no longer as long, rigid, or impractical as the exams of Imperial China, they are still difficult and important, and responsible for much of the stress faced by China's young. Examination month is known as "Black July."

Kao ya *(kow yah)* – Beijing duck or Peking duck, one of Beijing's most popular specialty dishes, also featured in many Beijing-style restaurants around the world...many of which (especially in Tokyo) feature China-trained chefs who create tastier Peking duck than their counterparts in China.

Laisee *(lie-suuh)* – These are red envelopes used to present "lucky money" to people as a gift. There are many occasions when money-gifts are the norm. Check with a Chinese friend if you are not sure that a money-gift is appropriate.

Lao *(lah-oh)* – Old. It is still a compliment to be called *lao* in China. Respect for the aged in China is not only steeped in the culture, it is also reflected in the law, the aged having many services and privileges denied to younger people.

Lian-ai *(lee-inn-aye)* – This is a new term, concocted in recent times, to mean romantic love between a man and a woman. In feudal China, the concept of romantic love was not unknown but it was not sanctioned by society and there was no word for it. This does not mean, however, that men and women in old China were not capable of romantic love and did not engage in it when the opportunity presented itself. However, there were few opportunities, at least for most people, because the two sexes were kept separated most of the time. On the other hand, sexual activity by itself was not regarded as a sin by the Chinese, and pornographic literature was popular during the long feudal age.

Liumang *(lee-uu-mahng)* – A term that originally meant "vagabond" but is now used to refer to the street hoodlums often seen in China's major cities. Combined with *shua (shua liumang)*, it is often used to describe the actions of a man deliberately feeling a woman on a crowded bus.

Luxinshe *(luu-sheen-shay)* – China Travel Service (CTS).

Mei-yu fa-zi *(may-yuu-fah-cee)* – "There is nothing you can do about it" or "It can't be helped," an expression that one often hears, especially in Taiwan, in reference to situations that actually cannot be changed or that appear hopeless. It may also be used as an excuse to avoid making any effort.

Mian'ao *(mee-in ow)* – The padded cotton coat that traditionally was so important to residents of northern China in winter.

Naixin *(nye-sheen)* – Patience…something foreigners are constantly being told they must have to get anything done in China.

Nei-hang *(nay-hahng)* – An expert, literally "inside the profession." By the same token, a novice is known as *wai-hang* or "outside the profession."

Nei wai yuobie *(nay wye yuu-oh-bee-eh)* – "Never forget there is a difference between Chinese and foreigners"—a common saying.

Pai-ma-pi *(pie-mah-pee)* – "Pat the horse's rump," an interesting way to say "brown-nose" or curry favor with someone.

Pa ma-fan *(pah mah-fahn)* – This literally means "to fear trouble," and is an expression the Chinese commonly use when they are afraid some action is likely to get them into trouble.

Renao *(ray-nah-oh)* – This is more or less the opposite of privacy, for which the Chinese originally had no word and little or no concept. By itself *renao* means "hot and noisy," and refers to the kind of relationships the Chinese have with family and friends, especially, when they are eating and drinking in public places.

Renminbi *(wren-men-bee)* – Literally "People's Money," *renminbi* is the national currency. It is broken down into ten jiao (jow) or mao (mow). There are ten fen (fun) to each jiao. Bills come in denominations of a hundred, fifty, ten, five, two, and one yuan; coins in five, two, and one fen.

Tong ju *(tong-juu)* – "Living in," a reference to a man and woman living together before they get married, a practice that became fairly common in China when men were not allowed to marry until they were 28 and women could not marry until they were 25. This was later changed to 22 for men and 20 for women.

Waiguoren *(wie-gwoh-wren)* – An "external country person," in other words a foreigner or what the Chinese call non-Chinese, with a neutral nuance. Also: *wai hang (wie hung)* or foreign businessman.

Wai bin *(wie bean)* or foreign guest; *waiguo pengyou (wie-gwoh pung-yoh-uu)* or foreign friend); *lao wai (lah-oh wie)*, a friendly term for foreigner; *da bizi (dah-bee-jee)*, a derogatory for foreigner.

Wan-sui! *(wahn-swee!)* – "10,000 years!" or "Eternal life!" This is the Chinese equivalent of Japan's *banzai*, and Britain's "Long live the king!" It is shouted on auspicious occasions as a grand gesture toward someone being honored.

Wei *(way)* – This is China's telephone "hello" and is more or less the equivalent of "yes" when it is used in answering the phone. Because of the vital importance of establishing respective social rank, protecting their "face," reluctance to get involved in new situations and identify themselves or their office directly and immediately over the phone, it often takes several *weis* before one succeeds in getting a conversation going, and the caller generally has to take the initiative.

Yang guizi *(whang gwee-jee)* – "Foreign devil"— what many Chinese used to call foreigners.

Yanjiu *(yahn-jew)* – "I'll / we'll study it." Another very common expression used to avoid making any kind of commitment. Often used with *kaolu*.

Youguan bumen *(yoh-uu-gwan buu-mane)* – "The concerned parties," an old expression referring to mystical "other people." Now used to refer to people without saying exactly who, as in "Gen youguan bumen lianxi" (Let's contact the concerned parties).

Zao-daisuo *(jah-ow die-suh-oh)* – Guest houses. The government maintains a large number of guest houses for use by high officials when they travel.

Zhongguo tong *(jong-gwah tong)* – "China expert," a compliment paid by Chinese to foreigners who show some knowledge of China.

Zidian *(cee-dee-inn)* – Dictionary. An English-Chinese dictionary that gives the Chinese equivalents in pinyin (Roman letters) can be very helpful to the visitor in China.

Zili-gengsheng *(cee-lee-gung-shung)* – Self-reliance, something that both Chinese and foreigners must have to live and work within the Chinese system.

PART SEVEN

Internet Gateways to China

PERSONAL AFFAIRS

Attorneys / Law Firms

http://www.lawyerinchina.net

http://www.lawyershf.com

Driver's Licenses / Driving Regulations

http://www.wikitravel.org/en/Driving_in_China#Laws

Export Laws

http://www.china.org.cn/english/travel/40407.htm

http://www.chinaexporthub.com/export-regulations/

http://www.nti.org/db/china/excon.htm

Foreign Embassies

http://www.embassiesinchina.com

Immigration Laws

http://www.chinatoday.com/law/IMMLAW.HTM

International Schools
http://www.english-schools.org/china/

Import Laws
www.china.visahq.com

Incorporation Laws
http://www.business-in-asia.com/china_invest_documents.html

Marriage Laws
http://www.procedurallaw.cn

National Holidays
http://www.chinaholidays.com

Requirements for Permanent Residence
http://www.china.org.cn/english/livinginchina/185007.htm

Visa Categories
http://www.china-embassy.org
http://www.visabureau.com
http://www.visarite.com/visaType.htm

BUSINESS-RELATED WEBSITES

http://www.allbusiness.com/first-business-trip-china/
Detailed information about the documentation needed for going to China as a businessperson; suggestions for hotel accommodations; advance preparations that you should make; how

to approach and engage in negotiations, and more. All of the contributors to the site are experts in their fields.

http://www.ChinaSolved.Com.
This is a group of Internet sites that are designed to provide the international business community with the resources they need to be successful in China as managers and leaders. The sites contain a wealth of practical advice obtained from long-time expatriate businesspeople in China.

http://www.internationalist.com/business/China
This is the website of *The Internationalist*, an online compendium of authoritative articles and columns by specialists in international business, trade, and investment in China.

http://www.Chinabusinessworld.com
This is a private commercial website that covers a variety of business-related topics on China, including relocation services, economic zones, trade shows, mailing lists, Chinese companies, U.S. companies in China, internship programs, business books, and information about traveling to China.

http://www.doingbusiness.org/data/exploreeconomies/china/
This huge site is maintained by The World Bank Group, and includes such things as detailed steps for starting a business in China, specific steps necessary to obtain construction permits (there are 27 steps), registering property, paying taxes, and more.

http://www.china-ready.com
Provides business strategies for China.

http://www.chinabig.com/en/market
Provides Chinese market information

CONSULTANTS

http://www.pwccn.com/home/eng
PricewaterhouseCoopersChina provides industry-focused assurance, tax, and advisory services.

http://www.cnfas.com
This site provides current information and analysis of Chinese food and agricultural markets.

http://www.uschinabiz.com
U.S./China Business Solutions offers information for American companies about outsourcing in China.

http://www.internationalist.com/business/China
Marketech China, a U.S.-China consulting group that specializes in the development and implementation of entry strategies for doing business in China.

LANGUAGE SITES

http://www.BizPanda.com
This site provides a comprehensive list of China's business terms.

http://www.ZapChinese.com
This site not only provides an extensive list of Chinese business terms, it also has an audio feature that gives the correct pronunciation of the terms.

http://www.GoogleTranslatc.Com

For instant translations of English and other language terms and sentences into Chinese, go to GoogleTranslate.com. This amazing system gives you the ideographic characters for single words and sentences as well as the *pinyin* (English phonetic) spelling of the terms. It also proves alternative meanings for individual words when they have more than one meaning.

Miscellaneous Information

———◦———

ENGLISH LANGUAGE PUBLICATIONS

China Daily
http://www.ChinaDaily.com.
This is China's national English language newspaper. Founded in 1981, it has a circulation of approximately one million.

China Post Online
http://www.ChinaPost.com.tw/
This is the online edition of Taiwan's leading English language newspaper.

China Today
http://www.ChinaToday.com
This site provides extensive information about China in Chinese and English, from the arts to who's who, plus numerous other sources.

The Economic Observer

http://www.eeo.com.cn/ (the Chinese edition)

http://www.eeo.com.cn/ens/ (the online English language edition)

This is a semi-independent weekly newspaper inspired by the U.K's *Financial Times* and considered by many to be one of the three top economic-focused newspapers in China. The paper has an online Chinese language edition and an English edition.

People's Daily Online

http://www.english.peopledaily.com.cn/

Launched in January 1998, People's Daily Online is a website maintained by *People's Daily*, the official newspaper of the Communist Party of China.

Shanghai Daily

http://www.ShanghaiDaily.com/

This site describes itself as the English language channel for news about China.

The Standard

http://www.thestandard.com.hk/

The Standard is a free English daily newspaper in Hong Kong. Audited daily circulation is approximately 250,000. It has evolved into an influential medium with a diverse audience and a broad reach since becoming free in September 2007. It is distributed Monday through Friday. It is also available in digital format across different media, including Apple iPad app, Nokia OVI app, and Facebook (www.facebook.com/thestandardhk). It delivers updated news to readers round the clock.

Asia Times Online
(English-language), Hong Kong
http://www.ATimes.com

China Labor Bulletin
(Independent English-language trade union journal)
http://iso.china-labour.org.hk/iso/

Far Eastern Economic Review
http://www.feer.com
Hong Kong, features in-depth articles about economic affairs in Asia.

Keji Ribao / Science and Technology Daily
http://www.stdaily.com
Government-owned, this publication features articles about science and technology in China.

Macau Daily Times
http://www.MacauDailyTimesnews.com/
(English-language), News about Macau.

South China Morning Post
http://www.scmp.com/
Published in Hong Kong, it features authoritative articles and analyses of business, political, and social affairs in Asia.

WEATHER PATTERNS IN CHINA

Weather patterns vary enormously across the country. Harbin in the far northeast is subject to bitterly cold winters, while Hong Kong and the Southeast have a subtropical climate and are hot and humid most of the year. One generalization holds true for much of eastern China—summers are hot, humid, and rainy. The best climate in China is found in Yunnan Province. Located in the South at a high elevation, Yunnan is pleasant the year round, but is rainy during the summer months.

Beijing
Beijing has extreme weather ranges from hot summer months comparable to those in the south, with the most rain in June and July. Winters are windy and often bitterly cold. Winters are also dry, with bright, sunny days and little snow. The capital and much of the rest of the eastern seaboard are subject to dust storms blowing in from the Gobi Desert.

Southern China
In the South, Guilin is rainy from April through June with hot, steamy summers. Winters can be quite cool.

Shanghai
Shanghai is cool to cold in winter, with hot and rainy weather during the summer.

Hong Kong
Hong Kong's weather is mainly hot and humid. The best season is from November to April when it is cool and dry. January and February can get quite chilly. However, temperatures

usually remain above 54º F (12° C). during this time with only a few days dropping to 46º F (8° C) or below.

Late February to the end of March, Hong Kong starts getting warmer and humidity begins to rise as the rainy season draws near. April to June are the wettest and most humid months.

July to September is typhoon season, with the temperature rising to as high as 93° F (34° C). This is the peak season for work holidays, and weather-wise it is not the best time to visit. October has warm days and cool evenings. Some rain can be expected but the temperatures and humidity levels begin to drop as the dry season sets in.

For current weather in China go to: http://www.weatherchina.org/.

Learning Some New Skills

————◦————

Many expatriate businesspeople stationed in China take advantage of the opportunity to experience and learn some of the customs and practices for which the country is famous. These include:

DAI JI JUAN (DIE JEE JWAHN) / THE GREAT ULTIMATE FIST

Visitors to China and other areas in Southeast Asia where there are large Chinese populations are seldom there for more than a day before they come across one or more Chinese engaging in a form of graceful exercise that resembles a slow-motion dance. The individual or individuals engaging in the exercise may be on a rooftop, in a small park, on a dock, or in some small secluded spot off the street. Wherever they are, the participants appear to be in a world of their own.

This distinctive Chinese practice, usually an early morning activity starting at sunrise, is known as *Dai Ji Juan* (Die Jee Jwahn) or "Great Ultimate Fist."

Legend has it that the theory behind the practice of *Dai Ji Juan* was conceived by a priest after watching a fight between a large bird and a snake. The snake avoided attack after attack just by moving its body in a carefully controlled weaving and waving manner. Finally, the bird tired, misjudged its timing, and became the victim of a lightning strike by the snake. (Chinese priests created a number of the best-known martial arts because they were prohibited from bearing arms and were subject to attacks by roadway bandits when traveling about the country.)

Dai Ji Juan consists of thirteen movements, eight with the arms and five with the legs, all performed slowly and with perfect balance, so that all the nerves and muscles of the body are brought into play. It stimulates the body and calms it at the same time, thereby promoting health and longevity. The exercise is said to be especially helpful in eliminating and preventing headaches, digestive problems, and rheumatism, and to be ideal for all ages, since it requires neither strength nor stamina. The movements of the arms are all circular as the body is gradually turned to eight points on the compass, which figuratively denote the cyclical changes in the cosmos and the evolution of nature.

Later disciples of *Dai Ji Juan* developed it into a martial art for use in fighting. The principle is to always retreat in the face of an attack and then to counterattack when the enemy overreaches himself. The body movements of the *Dai Ji Juan* fighter emulate those of the snake, keeping the adversary puzzled and denying any opportunity to strike a decisive blow.

Chinese practitioners of *Dai Ji Juan* are always willing to teach the exercise portion of the art. In fact, many people, foreigners included, are first initiated simply by showing up at a spot used by Chinese, taking a position a few yards away, and imitating the actions of the more skilled performers.

Foreign visitors in China (as well as Taiwan and Singapore) might take advantage of the opportunity to get some personal instruction in *Dai Ji Juan*–something that could well enhance both their mental and physical health and contribute to their establishing lifelong relationships with the Chinese.

ZHĒNJIŬ (JUNH-JEW) / ACUPUNCTURE

Foreigners in China who come down with some kind of physical complaint might also take advantage of the opportunity to try acupuncture. This form of treatment originated in China at least 2,500 years ago and is available in all modern Chinese hospitals today.

Acupuncture is based on inserting thin needles (now often stimulated with an electrical current) into "energy channels" on various places of the body to alter the flow and distribution of the energy to cure ailments as well as prevent them. There are said to be over 650 such "meridian points" on the body but only about a hundred of them are regularly used.

At this point, some Western medical authorities dispute the Chinese belief of "energy flow" in the body and the relationship of this flow with the health of the various body organs. Other Western doctors say, however, that acupuncture does appear to act as a painkiller.

Back in the mid-1900s a well-known *New York Times* journalist came down with appendicitis while he was in China. He underwent an operation in which only acupuncture was used to deaden the pain. He later wrote a glowing report on his experience, saying that he suffered absolutely no pain and that his recovery was faster than usual. His story resulted in the appearance of hundreds of acupuncture clinics across the United States in the following decade.

Acupuncture treatment for various problems generally consists of several sessions, depending on the nature and seriousness of the illness.

QIGONG (CHEE-GUNG) / DEEP BREATHING

Another skill that foreign visitors in China might find interesting is known as *qigong* (chee-gung) or "deep breathing." It is an ancient technique that is said to dramatically improve one's peace of mind, health, and longevity.

Qigong is also promoted as a technique for helping obese patients lose weight and thereby reduce high blood pressure.

Qigong dates from the period of Ze Dao in the seventh century B.C. It refers to the vital energy or "force" of life, which might be compared with electricity. Just as electricity gives "life" to a piece of mechanical or electronic equipment, *qi* does the same for the human body. Chinese scientists say they have not been able to explain *qi* through biological science, but that they believe it is a special form of energy.

Over the centuries, people who mastered the use of *qi* were able to achieve extraordinary mental and physical feats that go well beyond what is recognized or explainable by modern-day science—to the extent that during different ages, masters of the art were accused of being practitioners of black magic.

Chinese scientists have been trying since the 1980s to establish a scientific basis for the ancient practice of *qigong*, directed by the China Qigong Science Research Center in Beijing. A staff of *qigong* masters and scientists have also worked to develop the art into an independent science.

The leading advocates of *qigong* today are scientists, engineers, and medical doctors, instead of monks as in the old days. One such group of professionals in Beijing founded the private China Qigong Training (or Refresher) College, which is devoted to training *qigong* teachers. The college also sponsored the research and writing of ten textbooks covering the history, theory, and practice of *qigong*.

With an annual enrollment of some three hundred, the college has thousands of graduates who have set up schools in their own districts. Administrators at the college say they regard *qigong* as a national treasure and believe it will be at the forefront of life sciences in the 21st century. Millions of Chinese practice *qigong* daily and it is growing in popularity around the world.

Martial arts masters say it is the energy of *qi* that makes it possible for them to perform extraordinary feats, such as breaking a stack of several boards or bricks with a single blow of their bare hands.

The Tuttle Story: "Books to Span the East and West"

Most people are surprised to learn that the world's largest publisher of books on Asia had its humble beginnings in the tiny American state of Vermont. The company's founder, Charles Tuttle, came from a New England family steeped in publishing, and his first love was books—especially old and rare editions.

Tuttle's father was a noted antiquarian dealer in Rutland, Vermont. Young Charles honed his knowledge of the trade working in the family bookstore, and later in the rare books section of Columbia University Library. His passion for beautiful books—old and new—never wavered throughout his long career as a bookseller and publisher.

After graduating from Harvard, Tuttle enlisted in the military and in 1945 was sent to Tokyo to work on General Douglas MacArthur's staff. He was tasked with helping to revive the Japanese publishing industry, which had been utterly devastated by the war. When his tour of duty was completed, he left the military, married a talented and beautiful singer, Reiko Chiba, and in 1948 began several successful business ventures.

To his astonishment, Tuttle discovered that postwar Tokyo was actually a book-lover's paradise. He befriended dealers in the Kanda district and began supplying rare Japanese editions to American libraries. He also imported American books to sell to the thousands of GIs stationed in Japan. By 1949, Tuttle's business was thriving, and he opened Tokyo's very first English-language bookstore in the Takashimaya Department Store in Ginza, to great success. Two years later, he began publishing books to fulfill the growing interest of foreigners in all things Asian.

Though a westerner, Tuttle was hugely instrumental in bringing a knowledge of Japan and Asia to a world hungry for information about the East. By the time of his death in 1993, he had published over 6,000 books on Asian culture, history and art—a legacy honored by Emperor Hirohito in 1983 with the "Order of the Sacred Treasure," the highest honor Japan bestows upon non-Japanese.

The Tuttle company today maintains an active backlist of some 1,500 titles, many of which have been continuously in print since the 1950s and 1960s—a great testament to Charles Tuttle's skill as a publisher. More than 60 years after its founding, Tuttle Publishing is more active today than at any time in its history, still inspired by Charles Tuttle's core mission—to publish fine books to span the East and West and provide a greater understanding of each.